The
CALIFORNIA
LEMON LAW

WHEN YOUR NEW VEHICLE
GOES SOUR

HOW TO GET A REFUND OR ANOTHER VEHICLE WITHIN

60 DAYS

When Your New Vehicle Goes Sour

The CALIFORNIA Lemon Law Book

All fifty states now have 'Lemon Law' programs designed to help consumers with purchased or leased defective new vehicles. While not all programs are similar, most states have a no cost arbitration program as outlined within this book.

This book is written to help consumers understand the basic requirements of the 'Lemon Law' defective vehicle program in their state, how to qualify for 'Lemon Aide' and how to develop a strong case leading to a full and just award.

I have used the California 'Lemon Law' criteria as the baseline theme throughout the book basically because I know it best and it is the bedrock by which most other states have used to design their own laws. I have designated the last chapter of the book to contain the specific state statutes purposely, so the reader will already know what a DVU or MOF formula is before he finds it there.

Owning or leasing a defective vehicle that you paid considerable money for can be frustrating and exasperating in our busy daily lives. You can resolve this problem in the shortest possible time by reading this book. I know it will help you.

Joseph J. Caro

About the Author

Joseph J. Caro is a leading consumer arbitrator and mediator who has heard and reviewed hundreds of vehicle warranty cases over the past ten years. A member of the American Arbitration Association with a seat on the National Panel of Consumer Arbitrators, Joe is also listed in "Who's Who in the West" for his many outstanding contributions and accomplishments.

A long -standing consumer advocate, Joe has written several articles on the 'Lemon Law' and its application and benefit to the consumer. Joe was invited to participate in 'Lemon Law' regulation amendment hearings held by the California Department of Consumer Affairs. His suggested changes to this law and the certification process for manufacturer sponsored dispute resolution programs further aided the consumer.

ISBN 0-9628078-4-2 The California Lemon Law, When Your New Vehicle Goes Sour copyright 2003, Joseph J. Caro
Published by CCN Publishing P.O. Box 7486 Long Beach, CA 90807 all rights reserved.

Contact Joe Caro at: **lemonlawgoessour.com**

Contents

When Your New Vehicle
Goes Sour

Joseph J. Caro
Consumer Arbitrator/Mediator

Due to the overwhelming consumer demand for **When Your New Vehicle Goes Sour** 'Lemon Law' books, special editions have been printed for the following states. Contact your local bookseller or visit the web site at: **www. lemonlawgoessour.com** where you can download a copy.

Alabama	Maryland	Rhode Island
Arizona	Massachusetts	South Carolina
Arkansas	Michigan	South Dakota
California	Minnesota	Tennessee
Colorado	Mississippi	Texas
Connecticut	Missouri	Utah
Delaware	Montana	Vermont
District of	Nebraska	Virginia
Columbia	Nevada	Washington
Florida	New Hampshire	West Virginia
Georgia	New Jersey	Wisconsin
Idaho	New Mexico	
Illinois	New York	
Indiana	North Carolina	
Iowa	North Dakota	
Kansas	Ohio	
Kentucky	Oklahoma	
Louisiana	Oregon	
Maine	Pennsylvania	

OVERVIEW

You've purchased or leased a new vehicle and in spite of a five-year factory warranty it keeps breaking-down or is totally defective, undependable or worse—unsafe to drive! You have tried to have it fixed many times without success. You have been to the dealership so many times the Service Writer runs and hides when he sees you coming. The vehicle seemingly can't be fixed—but the payments still have to be made. You want to sue someone, *anyone* to restore your peace of mind—but you know it will cost a bundle!
Take heart, dear friend, relief is just a few pages away—
you can get a *new* vehicle or get your money back
within 60 days!
For *FREE!*

Since the inception of the new vehicle 'Lemon Law,' consumers have been guided by rumor and misinformation when faced with the possibility of owning a true 'Lemon.' In the twenty years that this law has been in effect, thousands of 'Lemon' owners have either lost valid cases or received far less of an award than they legally deserved. There are thousands more who owned 'Lemons' who would have applied for 'Lemon-Aide' had they known the law existed in the first place—but ended-up selling their vehicles at a loss or breaking their lease just to get rid of the nagging problem.

As a practicing consumer arbitrator/mediator who has worked with and specialized in Lemon Law cases for several years, I wrote this book as an easy-to-use guide to help you understand your 'rights' under applicable laws, to help you prepare your case and to win a fair and just award in as little as **60** days! You can do it yourself—you don't need a lawyer. This book gives you all the information you need.

CHAPTER ONE

The Lemon Law: What It Really Is

The advancement of modern technology has given us many wonderful features in today's automobile. Cars are not only much safer to drive, they are more fuel efficient, pollute less, handle better and have more comfort options than at anytime in the past. Today's automobile is truly a sophisticated engineering marvel . . . That is, until it stops working properly!

This book is designed as a self-help guide for those of us who have purchased or leased a motor vehicle (car, truck, SUV, RV) that for some unknown reason refuses to function as it should. The many trips to the dealership have ended in frustration on both sides of the repair counter and the problem or problems continue to exist. You are at an impasse. The dealer or service manager is sympathetic, but unable to solve the problem. What do you do? What *can* you do?

In the 1980's, many states passed into law a version of the Song-Beverly Consumer Act (California civil code § 1793.2) and the Tanner Bill (AB #2057). These separate legislative actions, when combined, form the foundation of the 'Lemon Law' relief program available to consumers. As simple and straight-forward as it may sound, gaining a meaningful 'Lemon Law' dispute resolution program was not easy to do. Substantial pressure from *all* auto makers have kept this program well hidden from the many consumers who would make good use of it.

While it's true that only a small fraction of the new vehicles that are sold throughout the country would classify as true 'Lemons,' estimates indicate that in California alone, there may be as many as 40,000 of these problematic vehicles on the road (sort of—when they run at all) of which 80% of the owners (about 32,000) will not file a claim for consumer relief under the state 'Lemon-Aide' program!! With the advent of home computers and the internet, more folks will know about 'Lemon Law'/ 'Lemon Aide' programs and will need this book to help them through the legalese and the forms.

This may sound confusing, but the 'Lemon Law' arbitration programs throughout the country are not automatic. This simply means no one will do it for you—and you must apply yourself. Your state Department of Motor Vehicles (DMV) in all likelihood, will have little idea of where to get the forms you need to use—or how to use them, if they could find them in the first place. The owner or lessee of the defective vehicle must shoulder the burden of proof that the vehicle *is* defective in the first place and submit the evidence of these facts in a proper manner, to the proper people who can help. Before we delve into the details of how this happens, I would like to first review the basic ABC's of how this book will help you:

        A. It will show how you basically qualify
        B. It will show how to prepare your case
        C. It will show you what to ask for
        D. It will show you how to ask for it
        E. It will show you how to get it

Consumer 'Lemon Law' programs in reality, are not the result of a single legislation but a combination of several laws and measures passed over a period of many years (at one time, new cars and vacuum cleaners had a similar guarantee period—90 days). The real foundation of all automotive warranty dispute laws began life at the federal level with the passage of the Magnuson-Moss Consumer Act which was followed a few years later by the Federal Trade Commission (FTC) enacting Rule # 703 which, generally speaking, allowed all consumer laws to be applied on a state-by-state basis.

In 1982 California passed the earlier mentioned Song-Beverly Warranty Act which brought forward specific elements of Rule #703 and in 1988 passed the Tanner Bill which additionally defined and modified the dispute resolution process *and* the arbitration process to make a fair and just program to help all consumers deal with 'Lemons' (there will be a test on this before mid-term break. Only kidding! The test will be *tomorrow*!).

The reason for all the law-passing in the mid-70's was simple when you looked at it. During this period of stringent federal EPA regulations, cars were getting more complicated to build. Long gone were the flat-head engines and gravity-fed fuel tanks. The advent of high technology, the need for clean air and overlapping technical automotive systems (smog pumps–catalytic converters, *et al)* led to mechanical problems that were difficult, if not impossible to trace, much less fix. It was when these assorted problems began to affect the safety and use of the vehicle that the lawmakers decided that something should be done to help their fellow taxpayer.

While the principal objective of this book is to provide you with the information and ability to effectively use the 'Lemon Law,' you must make a conscious effort to follow a specific course of action. Let's stop for a moment and examine the options that are open to you right now:

A. You could do nothing and live with the problem.

B. You could try to sell your 'Lemon' or trade it in on another car, which would in effect, pass the problem to someone as unsuspecting as you were.

C. Apply for relief under your state 'Lemon Law' program.

D. Hire an attorney and sue the manufacturer.

Okay, there they are. Pick the one you like best. If you selected option A or B . . . *Wrong!* You lose! Options A or B are just not practical because in both you assume the emotional and financial loss associated with owning a 'Lemon'. Option D may not be a great choice either: You may have to outlay a wad of cash to have the lawyer represent you, or if the lawyer works on contingency and wins—you may have to pay him around 40% of your settlement, meaning you still lose money on the deal. In some states, representation by an attorney may take more than a year to resolve— but you might still have to go to arbitration first!

There is a fifth option that I didn't mention on the previous page, which is to select the state certified arbitration hearing where you live *and* bring a lawyer! If you take this course of action chances are you will soon be at the door of option D anyway. Obviously I want you to select option C as the way out of the mess you're in—there are no legal fees and no long waits for justice. If you feel you need to bring Hank, your local mechanic to testify on your behalf as an 'expert witness' (just like on Perry Mason– or LA Law) that would be entirely up to you.

Remember one thing, if you think attending an informal case review or hearing would put butterflies in your stomach, you shouldn't worry, all state sanctioned 'Lemon Law' programs are specifically designed for the consumer and are very informal. By the time you and I have built a strong 'ironclad' case, your confidence will be so high you won't be able to wait for your hearing date!!

Simply stated, if you buy or lease a new motor vehicle and you find yourself having chronic problems with the operation of the vehicle *and* the problems meet the basic qualifications under the law, you may be entitled to a replacement vehicle or a refund of the purchase price! So, if your car, truck, RV or SUV was sold to you with the new vehicle warranty and if you operated this vehicle principally for personal or household purposes (non commercial), you then meet the basic qualifications.

Now let's take a look at other important criteria and various actual cases that fall within and outside the scope of the 'Lemon Law'.

CHAPTER TWO

Qualifying For 'Lemon-Aide'

Let's start this chapter by telling you what vehicles will *not* qualify for the 'Lemon Law' programs in most states. By the process of elimination, all the rest *do* qualify!

1. Motorcycles (all)

2. Motorhomes (except for chassis & engine)

3. Off-road or other non-registered vehicles

4. Vehicles used primarily for commercial purposes

5. Any vehicle with a gross weight in excess of 10,000 pounds

6. Vehicles purchased 'used' -unless it can be shown that the problem existed since the vehicle was new, or that the vehicle was sold with the remaining original new car warranty (extended warranties don't count).

Note: If you buy a new car in one state and move to another state, chances are your case will be heard under the laws of the state you're now living in– if you meet their 'Lemon Law' qualifications.

The 12/12 Problem:

Brought into law at a time when most new car warranties were 12 months or 12,000 miles, many state 'Lemon Law' programs still refer to this period as the 'basis time' of new car problems, even though the actual warranty extends to five years or more.

Simply stated, many states would only hear a case if the offending problem occurred within the first 12 months or 12,000 miles of ownership. Any problems past this period, many manufacturers state, is 'old news' and not covered—even if the original warranty was for three years or more!

California motorists will be pleased to know that I helped alter this clause during meetings with the California Department of Consumer Affairs to now cover the first 18 months or 18,000 miles. Folks living in other states may not be so lucky and should contact their Department of Consumer Affairs to find out. The following case study shows how the 12/12 clause worked—and why car makers wanted to keep it the way it was:

> John G. bought a Wombat Special that he uses for personal use and it came with a four-year, 40,000 mile factory warranty. John started having transmission problems at 10,000 miles and the dealership couldn't fix it after five times at bat. John has had enough and files for relief under the state 'Lemon Law' program. Question is: is he covered??

(*I told you there would be a test!*) . . . The answer from both views of the 12/12 clause was a resounding *YES!*

Now, let's take the same case study and start John's transmission problems at 14,000 miles and two -and one- half years into his warranty. Is he still qualified for relief under the 'Lemon Law'? After all, the factory warranty *does* cover his car for four years and 40,000 miles . . . right? Well, yes . . . and no! In many states where the 12/12 clause still may apply, the legal brains found a compromise and called it "presumption" - simply meaning that poor John G. would still have *some* sort of case when his transmission gave up the ghost at 14,000 but it would be substantially weaker because the "presumption" of the law (12 months, 12,000 miles) had expired. So Johnny boy would be awarded much *less* because the problem happened *after* 12,000 and *after* one year! God forbid that the problem happens when the car has 35,000 and 3 years nine months into his warranty –with the 'presumption' clause as it stands, he could possibly owe *them* some money!! (only kidding . . .now, isn't this *fun?*)

Don't be too concerned about being inside or outside of the legal "presumption" - this head-scratcher will be agonized over by the arbitrator or arbitrators hearing your case.

Now we will mosey over and see if your vehicle problems will actually qualify in the factory warranty corral.

Nuts & Bolts Basics:

Any mechanical problem or problems that you are having with your vehicle will qualify under the 'Lemon Law' if:

1. You can show that it is covered by the factory warranty:

2. The problems affect the value, use or safety of the vehicle:

3. A reasonable number of unsuccessful attempts have been made to fix it *or* the vehicle has been out of service for the repair of any number of problems for a total time amounting to 30 days or more in most states.

The above qualifiers are critical in establishing a valid case and are worth reading twice.

In order to clearly define what is meant by "a reasonable number of repair attempts" certain guidelines have been incorporated into your state 'Lemon Law' program.

To all intents and purposes, if you have reported *four* attempts to fix a major problem . . .you qualify!

If your vehicle was out of service for *30 days or more* in an attempt to fix any number of problems . . .you qualify!

A "reasonable" number of repair attempts is directly associated to the seriousness of the problem. If you experience total brake failure, you would think that one or maybe two attempts to fix it would be more than enough. If your car catches fire every time you start it, one failed repair attempt should do it.

The Four Repair Attempts:

If you have a serious problem with your vehicle that affects the value, use or safety that couldn't be repaired after four documented attempts, you have a strong case and don't have to worry about it being in the shop less than the stipulated 30 days. On the other hand, if you own what's called a 'Monday' vehicle, (one presumably made on Monday, after the assembly workers had a wild weekend) and it has all kinds of little aggravating problems that cause you to keep taking it back to the shop for . . .and ends up accumulating over 30 days there . . . you also have a strong case.

Limited vs. Implied Warranties:

The factory warranty that the dealership gives you is called a limited warranty, but in many states there is another warranty that also tags along known as an *implied* warranty! The formal name is *"implied warranty of merchantability and general fitness"*. This means that any new product sold in the state must be able to perform it's intended or advertised use. For example: The cell phone that you buy must be able to receive calls and allow you to call out. A tape recorder must be able to record and play back what it has recorded. A motor vehicle must provide safe and reliable transportation. While not generally stated within any written

warranties that come with all purchased items, your legal rights as a
consumer include all aspects of the
implied warranty, and this also includes your motor vehicle.

It's in the Book:

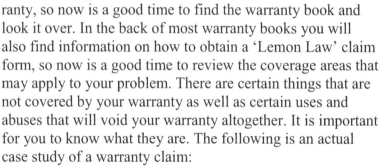

You should know that the problem
you are having is covered by the war-
ranty, so now is a good time to find the warranty book and
look it over. In the back of most warranty books you will
also find information on how to obtain a 'Lemon Law' claim
form, so now is a good time to review the coverage areas that
may apply to your problem. There are certain things that are
not covered by your warranty as well as certain uses and
abuses that will void your warranty altogether. It is important
for you to know what they are. The following is an actual
case study of a warranty claim:

**Case A. Abuse of the vehicle and use for other things
than intended.**
Customer used his new passenger car to pull-up tree
stumps at his mountain cabin and damaged the transmission and engine. This was seen to be abusive usage and
the warranty was rendered void.

Case B.
Customer experienced transmission failure while towing
a travel trailer. The trailer met the weight restrictions
found within the warranty and the owner won his case.

If, however, it could be shown that the owner towed the trailer at excessive speeds or it was found that the transmission was not properly maintained or the fluid level was very low, he would have voided his warranty and thereby lost his case for a new transmission.

You should realize by now that your entire case is based on the written factory warranty that came with your vehicle. If you want your case to be accepted for review you should clearly state that the problem *is* covered by the warranty, that the vehicle was purchased or leased principally for personal, family or household purposes (Also remember that the problem or problems with your vehicle must substantially reduce the vehicle's use, value or impact the safety of the vehicle. You will be asked to provide proof that there had been four or more repair attempts for a specific problem or the vehicle was out of service for 30 days or longer for miscellaneous repairs.

Lemon Law Check List:

Now is a good time to see just where you are in the 'Lemon Law' claims process. The following list will recap what we have covered so far and will give you the chance to review the necessary steps to building a case, which we will cover in the next chapter.

_____ You have purchased your vehicle mainly for personal use.

_____ Your vehicle has one or more problems that originated during the vehicle warranty period that you feel affects its value, use or safety. (Check your state's qualifiers in the last chapter)

_____ The dealership or authorized repair center has made at least four attempts to correct the problem (or less, if applicable) or your vehicle has been in the repair center for a cumulative 30 days or more.

_____ You have kept a list and record of all the repair attempts on the vehicle.

_____ You did not abuse the vehicle, or void the warranty.

_____ The problem (s) you are experiencing are covered under the factory warranty.

_____ The vehicle has been maintained according to the warranty.

CHAPTER THREE

Building a Winning Case

Before we begin building our 'ironclad' case, you probably would like to know if all this effort is worth it, in essence,
what you are allowed to receive if you win. While we will discuss this in the "Developing The Proper Award" chapter, you
may be entitled to the following:

A new replacement vehicle—similar to the model giving
you problems, with similar factory accessories.
Or
you will be granted the original purchase price - your
choice.

Any costs you have personally expended on the vehicle,
ie: towing, rental car, sales taxes paid for the vehicle, license fees and in some cases, interest charged on the
loan, also qualify.

It is doubtful that you will be awarded punitive damages,
multiple damages or other consequential damages, nor attorney fees in most states.

In California and many other states, the arbitration process
is voluntary, and non-binding, unless you agree with the case
results. If you don't agree with the arbitrator's findings you
are still free to hire a lawyer and proceed with a civil action
against the manufacturer.

The next step in your 'Lemon Law' action requires some
information gathering and letter writing to build the strongest
case possible.

It is important that you have in your possession all the repair orders (RO's) directly dealing with the vehicle problem. If you don't have them, or are missing a few, ask the repair facility that worked on your vehicle for copies. They will be glad to help you. Remember, your claim is not against the dealership—it's against the manufacturer. Also keep in mind that the auto maker is not willingly going to cut you a fat check. You must build your case first and document it with evidence.

Document Everything:

As the old story goes . . . It's easier to get a divorce in California than get rid of a Lemon! So you can't leave holes in your documentation evidence large enough for your award to fall through. Don't forget receipts for other collateral costs; towing, car rental, sales tax, other related repair costs paid, etc.

If at all possible, arrange your paperwork dealing with the problem into a logical sequence of events starting with when the problems first began. If you are in a car pool and riders in your vehicle experienced the problem, you should ask them to write a letter with that information. Make sure they put the date of the occurrence, the time, and any other pertinent information. Have them sign it and list their address and phone number. If you really want to look in-charge of your case, have the witnesses' letters notarized.

Remember, the repair orders (RO's) are key in your document list. They contain all the necessary information to substantiate your case. If you took your vehicle into the shop because it was leaking oil, and that developed into the major problem your case is founded on, then that would be the starting repair order. Don't take *all* your paperwork . . . just what can be used as evidence supporting your claim. If you took your vehicle in to repair the oil leak and they couldn't find it, or repair it, you want to bring that RO as well.
Remember what you are trying to prove: four or more repair attempts on a serious problem, or 30 days or more in the shop for a variety of problems! Arrange your data accordingly.
The two worst things you can say at the hearing are: "I know I have it somewhere . . ." or, "Gee, I just can't seem to find it. I must have left it home."

Start a File:

When you have your papers in order you should write a polite letter to the manufacturer explaining the problem. You will find the address in the back of the warranty book. Remember, the dealer can't help you at this point, so there is no reason to vent and yell at him! The folks at the manufacturer you will want to contact will either be Customer Relations Department; Complaint Appeals Board or the Alternate Dispute Resolutions Department.

In some cases there will be a toll-free number in the warranty book that you can call to request the proper forms. Again, be polite. Save your energy for the hearing.

Once you have decided to take a 'Lemon Law' action because of your problems, don't waste a lot of time harping on the dealership about it. If they could have helped you, they already would have. It simply is out of their hands. I suggest that you continue to have the offending vehicle (if it's still running) serviced at the dealership while you await the scheduling of your case under the 'Lemon Law'. Directing your attention to the manufacturer at this point, brings you one step closer to getting your vehicle properly repaired, having it replaced or getting a refund.

Letter Format:

When you write to the manufacturer, or directly to the Dispute Resolution Program in your state, keep it simple, to the point and above all, civil! The content of this letter certainly is no place to vent your built-up frustrations caused by the 'Lemon' parked in your driveway. You are now in the realm of paper-pushers who don't have a personal interest in you, your vehicle or what you have to say. As Jack Web from the old 'Dragnet' television show was fond of saying (remember him?) "Just the facts . . . Ma'am, Just the facts."

In some cases, the form the manufacturer sent you to complete may be a single printed page with just a line or two for you to include any "comments." I personally think the auto makers attempt to restrict your "comments" to a line or two, is on purpose. I strongly suggest that after you complete the form they sent you, that you attach a copy of the letter which you sent them, thoroughly explaining in detail, all the problems you have experienced. This gives you the opportunity to state your case adequately and have it attached to the form.

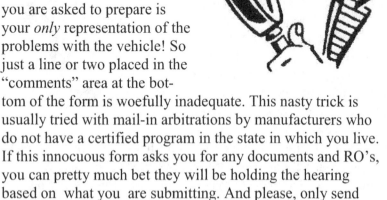

There are several cases that have come to my attention where the "standard" form you are asked to prepare is your *only* representation of the problems with the vehicle! So just a line or two placed in the "comments" area at the bottom of the form is woefully inadequate. This nasty trick is usually tried with mail-in arbitrations by manufacturers who do not have a certified program in the state in which you live. If this innocuous form asks you for any documents and RO's, you can pretty much bet they will be holding the hearing based on what you are submitting. And please, only send them copies . . . never originals!

Example Letter Format:

Ed Sell Motors, Inc, LLC, LTD
Los Angeles, CA 90800

Dear Sir/Madam:

This letter is to inform you that I am most dissatisfied with my recently purchased (make, model and VIN number of vehicle).

After taking delivery of this vehicle (you can say car, truck, RV if you want to) from (agency/dealership, with address) on (date) and driving it for less than (approx. miles driven before the problem) I encountered repeated problems with (list problems).

The people at (agency/dealership) have tried to fix these problems (number of repair attempts) without success. (**Or** you can state here) The car has been in the shop for a total of _____ days and the continuing problems with the vehicle, in addition to being an inconvenience, in my opinion, affect the value, use and safety of the vehicle (only use the ones that apply).

I therefore request, under the (your state) Lemon Law that this vehicle be replaced or a full refund awarded to me, in addition to related costs I have incurred since the problem existed. An itemized list of these costs are: _____

Thank you for your cooperation in this matter.

I *strongly* recommend that you attach a copy of this problems/application letter to *any* forms that you mail back to the manufacturer or a dispute resolution program handling your case (sometimes just an internal office of the auto maker). Some programs that are run by the auto maker themselves, may hold a hearing and make an "award" solely based on the information you sent them (if it's to their advantage) so if you don't include the incidental and collateral expenses (sales tax, towing, car rental, etc.) you probably won't be getting reimbursed for them!

Further on in the book we will fully cover both incidental and collateral expenses and you will be very surprised just how much money it cost you to drive your 'Lemon;' and you will realize just how sweet the 'Lemon Aide' will taste when you get your settlement check in the mail!

CHAPTER FOUR

Dispute Resolution Programs

I have mentioned the term 'Dispute Resolution Programs' several times in the book already, and you have probably heard this term bandied about at the 19th Hole at your local country club. Well, put your putter back in the bag and roll-up your mental sleeves because we are going to cover the topic—and yes, there will be a test!

Back in chapter one I mentioned the Magnuson-Moss Warranty Act of 1975 as pretty much laying out the ground rules and foundation for the 'Lemon Law' to follow. When the FTC (Federal Trade Commission) established Rule #703, the groundwork was complete for setting the parameters for the process known as Dispute Resolution. Rule #703 had in effect, become the 'vehicle' (excuse the pun) by which any state government could establish and structure a meaningful resolution program in a fair and just way.

The fact is, that prior to the 1983 consumer laws, in many states the only recourse that the owner of a defective vehicle had, was (to the joy of most lawyers) to take the manufacturer to court. Which then, as now, was an expensive, time consuming process. With the inclusion of the FTC's Rule #703 in many state consumer programs, laws regarding defective vehicles are now enforceable and monitored within state certified dispute programs.

Offered as a viable alternative to costly litigation, 'Lemon Law' resolution programs were designed to be offered free-of-charge to all consumers who qualify.

The agreement that was struck between the manufacturers and most states, said that if the manufacturer participated and paid for the operation of a state 'certified' dispute resolution program in cases involving their vehicles, they would be insulated, to a certain degree, from direct consumer litigation and *treble* punitive damages (which is often the result of private court claims). This new compromise installed a sort of legal 'buffer zone' between the consumer lawyers and car makers—who thought it was a nifty idea. Now, that's not to say that the consumer couldn't sue the manufacturer directly—they could! They just had to go through the dispute resolution program first.

Dispute resolution programs are known by several names or AKA's- (also known as) like Mafia members in the old days; Antonio Marjuleinni, aka: "Tony the Toilet," "Flat-nose Tony" etc. (I'm Italian, so I hope I can get away with this). The following terms and aka's principally mean the same thing: arbitration!

Consumer Warranty Program
Automotive Dispute Resolution
Independent Dispute Resolution
Third Party Dispute Resolution

Whatever the terminology used, arbitration, in my opinion, is the most effective means to settle product related conflicts between the customer and the manufacturer without resorting to litigation – or calling "Tony the Toilet" to resolve the problem.

The Process:

In fashioning Rule #703 the Federal Trade Commission was concerned that the program and process should not be so complex that individual consumers could not use it without professional help. The single overriding intent of Rule #703, was to avoid creating artificial and unnecessary procedural burdens, so long as the basic goals of speed, fairness and independent objectiveness continued to be met. The sole purpose of informal dispute settlement mechanisms was designed to simplify and expedite the resolution of warranty disputes.

The Arbitrator:

A quick summary of the FTC's arbitrator guidelines:

"An independent person or panel who are interested in a fair and expeditious settlement of the dispute, are independent of the parties to the dispute, and will not have any involvement in the making, distributing or servicing of any product."

Section Review
(I *told* you there would be a test!)
Action Plan:
Let's take a minute to develop a personal check-list of what we have covered so far . . .

1. By now, you should have a file developed of all attempted repair information (RO's too) and correspondence about the vehicle. If you read or hear anything about a re-call of your make vehicle for similar problems, obtain copies of this important information for your file as well.

2. You should have already written the manufacturer asking to enter the dispute program. If there is a toll-free number to call, you should do so, in addition to mailing the letter.

3. You should have copies made of everything! RO's, repair information, letters from witnesses, letters and forms sent to the auto maker, towing bills, etc.

4. You have used caution, caution, caution when you completed what seemed to be a 'standard' form sent to you for case information by the auto maker—especially if you are asked to *sign* the paper! Remember, some wiley auto makers have been *known* to disguise the 'agreement to arbitrate' to appear like a simple, innocuous application! If any part of the form asks you to "describe what you would like done to resolve your problem" ***watch out!*** They could use this form as your signed agreement to arbitrate ***without you being there!***

Steps to Arbitration:

In California, and most other states, the auto maker is encouraged to meet with you to try to resolve the problem before an arbitration hearing. They realize that it is to their advantage to do so because they know the law and the position they're in, and they hope you don't. Here is some important information covering all pre-arbitration contact.

A. If the manufacturer requests a meeting to discuss the problem, I encourage you to attend. If there is a third party present however, you should ask if it is a mediation hearing. Sometimes a mediation hearing is used by the auto maker to try to resolve the case before arbitration—usually they try to get you to take less than may be awarded by the actual arbitration hearing.

B. If you attend such a meeting and don't come to an agreement or settlement, you should inform the auto maker's representative at the meeting that you are requesting an arbitration hearing of this case under the laws of your state.

C. In all states, there are three types of arbitration hearings:
The oral hearing , which is conducted in person.
The written hearing, which you do not attend.
The telephonic hearing, which is a conference call between all parties at a scheduled time.

(I personally feel that the oral hearing gives you the best opportunity for a fair case. In my opinion, the best decisions and awards come from the oral, in-person hearings).

D. If after the hearing (the decision takes approximately 10 days) you find that you do not agree with the arbitration decision, all is not lost! You can still contact your attorney and file a civil claim. If you feel however, that the hearing was conducted improperly, you should contact your Department of Consumer Affairs and report your claim and reasons.

Note: In California, and other states, the arbitration decision that is made in your case is binding on the manufacturer . . . but *not* on you! Unless of course, you decide to accept the decision, then, it's binding on everybody. This means that the auto makers have agreed in advance, to give you the opportunity to accept the decision, or to reject it and maybe file a civil action. You should also know that if you do decline the hearing decision and proceed to a civil court, the fact that you turned down the arbitration decision can be admissible as evidence against you.

So How Good Are These Programs Working?

Glad you asked . . .statistics show that in New York and Massachusetts for example, awards made in favor of the consumer have been running at 68% or higher! This is a mighty strong statement for the fairness of arbitration settlement programs in general.

You may also like to know that while the 'Lemon Law' allows for a replacement vehicle or a refund, 93% of the cases awarded in the above two states elected for a refund rather than a replacement vehicle.

CHAPTER FIVE

Developing a Proper Award

In this chapter we will examine various types of awards under the 'Lemon Law,' and look at good and not-so-good decisions made by arbitrators. We will look at: restitution awards–replacement vehicle awards—and incidental/collateral damages.

Replacement Vehicle Awards:

In the event that you decide to accept a replacement vehicle rather than a refund, this is how the 'Lemon Law' explains your rights:

"In the case of replacement (vehicles), the manufacturer shall replace the buyer's vehicle with a new motor vehicle, substantially identical to the vehicle replaced. The replacement vehicle shall be accompanied by all express (written) and implied warranties that normally accompany new motor vehicles of that specific kind. The manufacturer also shall pay for, or to, the buyer the amount of any sales or use tax, license fees, registration fees, and other official fees which the buyer is obligated to pay in connection with the replacement, plus incidental damages to which the buyer is entitled to under Section §1794(California), including but not limited to, reasonable repair, towing and rental car costs actually incurred by the buyer."

Restitution Awards:

In cases where the consumer is requesting a refund award from the manufacturer, most laws are quite clear on
what is to be done:

*"The manufacturer shall make restitution in an amount
equal to the actual price paid or payable by the buyer, including any charges for transportation and manufacturer
installed options, but excluding non-manufacturer items installed by a dealer or the buyer, and including any collateral
charges such as sales tax, license fees, and other official
fees, plus any incidental damages to which the buyer is entitled under Section §1794 (California), including but not limited to: reasonable repair, towing and rental car costs actually incurred by the buyer."*

It's hard to imagine a statement of law being any clearer. It
describes exactly what is, and what is not to be included in
awards for replacement vehicles or refund of monies paid. In
spite of the fair (and clear) statements presented in this law,
there are perhaps thousands of consumers in your state who
walk away from the arbitration hearing table accepting thousands of dollars *less* than they are entitled to receive!!

This happens when arbitrators and consumers alike, fail to
do their homework, or fail to ask for, or judge the proper
award that is clearly allowed under the law. We will now
look at a few case studies covering both award hearings.

Vehicle Repurchase: Case Study

In an 'oral hearing' case that I attended as one of a three member arbitration panel, the consumer presented a strong case on her behalf. She submitted supportive documents to her case and other files and information that allowed us to make a two-to-one decision in her favor, and to order the offending vehicle repurchased. The other two panel members refused, however, to allow her incidental damages claim to stand for the rental car that she used while her 'lemon' was in the shop. They also refused to consider reimbursement for sales taxes and state registration fees.

While I argued that clearly under the law she was due this reimbursement, they decided two-to-one against me, stating that they were unable to grant the repayment of stated damages because the consumer did not specifically request the Resolution Panel to hear evidence in that regard, and there were no submitted receipts attached when she filed her claim.

The award portion that was denied totaled over $2,000!

Remember: If You Don't Ask For It—You Won't Get It!

Vehicle Repurchase: Case Study II

Sitting on a panel of three arbitrators in an 'oral hearing' claim against a major manufacturer, the consumer presented undeniable evidence and records and files and the case was judged in his favor. The decision was to repurchase the vehicle in question. Things went well in the award deliberations meeting of the Arbitration Panel until the question of 'discounted value of use' was discussed.

Note: The term *"Discounted Value of Use"* is generally applied to repurchase awards and simply means that the consumer is obligated to pay for (or not to receive payment on) that portion of use that he/she had of the vehicle, before the serious problem leading to the judgment became apparent. In other words, if you had trouble-free driving for 4,000 miles before the key problem began, then you would be obligated to pay for that specific amount of usage (many states have different stipulations).

In the case before me, the consumer presented repair orders and other evidence indicating the problem first began at 7,542 miles, which was listed and recorded on the repair order (RO) from the dealership. During the mandatory vehicle inspection by the arbitration panel (in cases of repurchase we actually had to inspect the vehicle in question) it was noted that the vehicle presently had 16,850 miles on the odometer and was listed on the inspection form. During our deliberations on the "discounted value of use" segment of award considerations, I was outvoted that the mileage use would reflect 16,850 miles as "discounted value of use" instead of the 7,542 miles allowed by law. I was again outvoted when it came to establishing the cost of this usage figure. The rate of .20 cents-per-mile was selected by the other Panel members (at that time, this was a very high rate) and the discounted value of use was established as $3,370.00 which was deducted from the award. Using the proper math set by law, the 'cost of use' equation in this case would only have been $1,508.40 (based on 7,542 miles) reflecting a savings (or gain) to the consumer award of $1,861.60!

If the consumer had known the application of "discounted value of use" he
could have appealed his case—and won!
The state of California has amended this
section of the 'Lemon Law' dealing with
the "use" award. It is now called:
*"Mileage Offset Formula" and works
like this:
Purchase price x miles driven
                120,000

So, if you paid $19,500 for your vehicle and drove it 9,500
before the problem became evident, then your "mileage offset" or discounted value of use would be:

$19,500. X 9,500 = $1,544.00
       120,000

This segment of the award would
then reflect the following:
$19,500. Minus $1,544. = $17,956.00
*Source: California Civil Code Section
1793.2 (d)(2)(C)

When a manufacturer repurchases a problematic or defective vehicle, the law clearly states that the buyer shall only be liable to pay for the amount directly attributable to use (*miles you drove the vehicle before it fell apart*) prior to the time you brought it back to have *the* problem repaired that led to the non-conformity of the vehicle (*when it turned into a LEMON!*).

The section goes on to state that, when restitution is made by the manufacturer, the amount to be paid to you, will be reduced by the amount of driving you did (*before the wheels and other important parts fell off!*) prior to the time you took it in.

Okay, . . . now here's the fun part! Put on your math caps!
(see, I told you there would be a test!)

The California Civil Code additionally states that, the amount directly attributable to use by the buyer, shall be determined by *multiplying* the actual price of the new motor vehicle (paid for, or payable) including any transportation charges and manufacturer's options, by a *fraction* having as its denominator, the number 120,000 . . .and as its numerator, the miles traveled *before it fell apart - (take two aspirin, and call me in the morning).*

So, if we take the previous Case Study and use the actual miles driven prior to *"the problem"* of **7,542** miles and used it as the *numerator* as the Code suggests, and use the *denominator* of **120,000** as suggested (*which, by the way, represents the expected total mileage a non-lemon car will travel before it totally falls apart, except in New York and other states where expected lifetime mileage is only 100,000)* we should be left with: **0.06285**. Which is meaningless, until it is *multiplied* by the price of the vehicle, which in this Case Study was: **$16,550.00** and the math would go like this:

16,550 x 0.06285 = 1,040.16

(which is the computation of both the DVU and MOF formulas and extrapolates the amount that will be deducted from your award, which is: **$1,040.16**)

Note: When you divide the miles driven by this amount, you are left with the mileage cost of a reasonable **13.7 cents-per-mile.**

If the arbitrators in the Case Study would have correctly used the MOF (mileage offset formula) as is shown above, and as described in the 'Lemon Law,' the consumer would have gained an *additional* **$468.24** to his settlement! (don't believe me? Check the math)

"I am the denominator . . . I will be *back!!!"*

Knowing the formulas used in deciding the award amount due you and *how* to use them is critical! I just want to remind you of one thing :

**"If you don't know what constitutes a good award . . .
How will you know when you are given a bad one?"**

I have scripted an actual "Lemon Law Test Case" that will take you from the onset of vehicle problems, the case filing, the evidence, arbitration, decision, and case computation. I call it: *"Billy Buys a Turbo Toad"* (look for it in a theatre near you this summer).
This case will give you the practice you need to build your own "ironclad" case.
While it is the arbitrator's job to know and apply the state 'Lemon Law' codes in your case, I highly recommend that you know them too. After all, it is *your* money!

"Billy Buys A Turbo Toad"

We find our young hero, Silly Billy Bland, walking the two miles from the Turbo Toad Emporium to his job, where he works as an assistant brain surgeon. His newly purchased car, a Turbo Toad Deluxe XV-2, is sitting in the shop again, with the same problem that has plagued the car since it reached 3,000 miles. This is the fifth time he brought it back in the last three months, he thought to himself as he sadly trudged down the street, thinking how he could just kick himself for paying so much money for it. After all, assistant brain surgeons really don't make *that* much money, not yet, anyhow. Billy recalls how happy he was when he paid $14,560 out-the-door; which included a $1,000 factory sun roof and $600 in transportation charges. Other extra hidden charges Billy had to pay included registration fees, sales tax, and finance charges on the loan he made.

Thinking that his car problems were never going to end, Billy wrote the manufacturer and they sent him his 'Lemon Law' form . . . which asked for the current mileage, which by now was 9,500 miles. Billy also sent back copies of repair orders clearly showing the problem began at 3,000 miles.

Billy dutifully completed the section of the form which asked him what he would like done about the problem. He quickly wrote that he would like the purchase price refunded, which was $14,560 and sent the form to the manufacturer. Billy happily returned to his job as an assistant brain surgeon, expecting to be notified when his case was ready for hearing. A few weeks went by and one day Billy opened his mail and found that he had been sent an "award decision" in his 'Lemon Law' case! The letter informed him that he had won! The letter also stated that he would be contacted by the car maker to turn in his Turbo Toad and then receive a check in the amount of $11,060. He was further informed that the sun roof and transportation costs were deleted from his award, and he was charged .20 cents-per-mile for the miles used (9,500) which came to $1,900.

Billy decided that, while he maybe could have done better with the award, he felt that *"half a loaf was better than none"* and he wanted to cut his losses and aggravation, and get on with his life.

Question: Was this a fair award? Was it a proper DVU or MOF? (mileage offset formula).

Answer: *Of course not!*

Lets look at the MOF assessment as starters: The car maker charged Billy the use of the vehicle for the full 9,500 miles on the odometer with a base of .20 cents-per-mile adjustment, nicking his award by $1,900. If Billy would have bought this book, he would have known that he would only pay for 3,000 miles of use, and not the full mileage of 9,500. He would have also known the formula: 3,000 miles divided by 120,000 would equal .025 times the purchase price of $14,560. And the sum of $364 would be the assessed use, and *not* $1,900 as claimed by the car maker. This small calculation would have added to Billy's award the amount of: **$1,536.00!!**

Lets take a peek at the other award aspects to see if any additional gain to Billy's award could have been made.
When Billy filled out the 'Lemon Law' form he should have listed the purchase price of the Turbo Toad as:

$12.960.   Base price
$ 1,000.   Sun roof option
$ 600.   Transportation charges
$14,560. Total Purchase Price

He should have listed other costs associated with his purchase:

Collateral Charges:

The 'Lemon Law' in California (and other states) allows the consumer to receive *"collateral charges"* incurred that relate to his purchase. Billy forgot that he had paid for the following:

$873.00 sales tax
$357.00 registration fees
$165.00 license fee
$100.00 smog certificate
$1,495.00 Total Collateral Charges

Which, when added to the total purchase price of the vehicle ($14,560.00) now shows a total amount of: $16,055.00 that Billy actually invested in the Turbo Toad! When we deduct the MOF (mileage offset formula) of $364.00 we now see that Billy's award should have been **$15,691.00** and not the $11,060.00 offered by the car maker!

Incidental Damages:

Many state Civil Codes mandate that in addition to other consumer incurred expenses, those having incidental impact to the vehicle must also be considered:

$175.00 rental car costs (while his Toad was in shop)
$125.00 towing charges
$ 75.00 emergency road service
$780.00 extended warranty cost
$250.00 pre-payment penalty—or loan origination fee
    on car financing.
$1,405.00 Incidental Damages

The incidental damages amount ($1,405.00) is then *added* to the adjusted total purchase price of $15,691.00 and gives us, under the law, **a realized award of $17,096.00!!** which is a far cry from the $11,060.00 that Silly Billy accepted because he wanted to: "*save time and get on with his life.*" He actually left **$6,036.00** of *his* money in the bulging pockets of the manufacturer!

How can they get away with such a thing?? Isn't that illegal?

Auto makers are not doing anything illegal when they offer you a settlement that is considerably less than you have a right to receive—and you accept it! Some call it the "Art of Negotiation," but the fact is . . . if they know the ins and outs of the 'Lemon Law' and you don't, you will probably accept far less than your state civil code authorizes.

Your only defense is knowing what your 'Lemon Law' rights are . . . and how to get them!!

By understanding the basic structure and intent of your state 'Lemon Law' program, you can now see how vulnerable your case might be! This is not to say that case arbitrators or arbitration panels purposely make improper awards, because they don't. They are a fine and honorable group of well-trained individuals who have dedicated much time to accurately resolve cases of this sort. Much of the problem lies in "dispute review programs" sponsored by the auto makers themselves.

CHAPTER SIX

Clear Title

When a consumer seeks to have his/her 'Lemon' repurchased by the manufacturer and the arbitrator so awards, it is up to the consumer to provide clear title/ownership papers to the manufacturer when the vehicle is returned. This provision has created headaches for many consumers who have financed the vehicle and therefore cannot produce the clear title needed. There are several solutions:

Manufacturer sponsored financing like GMAC, for example, (General Motors vehicles) are the easiest to handle. All the consumer must do is to write a letter to the place of payment, sending a copy of the arbitration decision and stating the need for a clear title to the vehicle. The folks at these inhouse lending agencies will usually arrange an internal transfer of all necessary paperwork and will issue a check when the vehicle is delivered to the representative.

If the vehicle was financed through a commercial bank or S&L, the consumer may be asked to do one of two things: sign a personal note on the balance owed, or provide other collateral (similar value or higher) until balance is paid.

You won't be able to get a two-party check (in most states) from the car maker to you *and* the lender. At this writing, there is no provision for anything other than the stated requisite of "providing a clear, unencumbered title."

The Warranty Paradox:

Earlier in the book we talked at considerable length about the 'Lemon Law' 12/12 clause and "presumption" that often confused both law makers and consumers alike. The following stipulations to the 12/12 clause and "presumption" are excerpted from the California Department of Consumer Affairs and was written by their legal department. It is a slight turnaround from previous policy and certainly worth your attention because, it may be to your advantage to know it!

"The scope of a program that is the subject of the bureau's certification process therefore extends to all* disputes involving performance under written warranties on new motor vehicles. These include not only those complaints which are the subject of the presumption* of the new car "Lemon Law" (those in which the manufacturer has made four or more repair attempts, or the vehicle has been out of service for a cumulative total of more than 30 calendar days during the first year or 12,000 miles of operation and the nonconformity substantially impairs the vehicle's use, value or safety) but also complaints involving the manufacturer's performance under written warranties whose duration exceeds one year* or in which the nonconformity does not substantially impair use, value or safety."

What they are saying is you can still have a strong case for a major problem *after* 12 months or 12,000 miles *and* a strong case for many minor problems that lead to 30 days in the shop . . . throughout the *entire* warranty period set by the manufacturer on that vehicle!

This Civil Code section sums it up quite nicely with the following: *"if an automobile manufacturer offers a longer written warranty (for example 5 years) and during this period is unable to service or repair the vehicle to comply with the warranty after a reasonable number of attempts, the manufacturer is obligated* to either replace the vehicle or make restitution."*

A few paragraphs later we find the civil code dealing directly with "presumption:" (There is no test . . . But it *is* very important reading!)

. . ."this obligation exists without regard to whether the one year or 12,000 mile limitation has been exceeded (Civil Code §1793.2(d)) (California). The one year 12,000 mile limitations only apply to the application of the presumption of the new car Lemon Law* (Civil Code §1793.2(e). If the duration of a written warranty is five years, and the problem first occurs more than one year after delivery, the presumption will not be available, but the buyer still may have a right to restitution or a replacement if the manufacturer has been unable to honor the terms of the warranty after a reasonable number of attempts."

The above statements and others found within this important consumer document have been undersigned by the Supervising Legal Council of the Department of Consumer Affairs (California) and clearly show that the consumer has gained some ground in the eyes of the state. The manufacturer's case is a bit weaker because the 12/12 clause itself, is a bit weaker.

Legal Help?

 One of the most frequently asked questions about 'Lemon Law' cases is the question about the need for professional legal help in the development or presentation of the case. This is a decision that only the consumer can answer, but there are a few things that must be considered before a decision is made:

The 'Lemon Law' program and process was specifically designed so that the average consumer can effectively represent his/her case and provide the necessary documentation. Case arbitrators are specially trained to help the consumer feel at ease in an informal setting (usually an office conference room) and will gently ask the consumer questions to fully understand the case, the majority of which has already been submitted in the case file and related documents. The entire case will stand alone, based on the thoroughness of case preparation. There is not a lot of speaking going on in an arbitration hearing from either side of the table. There are no case "summaries" to prepare, nor specific laws or "case files" to quote from. The next chapter will cover all the physical aspects of a hearing and what it entails. In my opinion as an arbitrator, the average consumer can do a remarkably fine job without legal help.

You should also remember that, in most states, you retain the right to reject the arbitrator's decision (the decision is mailed to you 10 days or so after the hearing) and file a civil case, where legal representation would be warranted.

Most 'Lemon Law' cases are represented by the owner of the offending subject vehicle, but many states allow the consumer to bring someone to help represent their case if they wish. A friend, relative, neighbor or even a lawyer.

The two main elements that you really need to know to structure a winning case are: proper documentation of your files that clearly show the vehicle is defective under the 'Lemon Law' . . . and a good understanding of the content of this book.

For consumers who may still feel a little unsteady in going it alone, there is another alternative that will also work well; have your family lawyer review your case with you before your arbitration hearing date. There are three main areas where experienced or legal help may be beneficial:

Initial Case Review:

Where a more objective mind may help you determine if you actually have a case based on the basic requirements outlined within this book.

Case Preparation:

Someone to help you actually structure your case documentation files; letters, repair orders, incidental costs and expenses, etc. and perhaps, help you file the initial form.

Representation:

Someone to go with you to the hearing, or be with you during telephone meetings, or the telephone hearing itself.

There are no legal restrictions preventing a professional consumer mediator/arbitrator to help you prepare your case. With the advent of home computers and the internet, distance is no longer a problem to hold case-related meetings and evaluate pertinent information. I have personally helped many consumers structure their "ironclad" cases and occasionally represented their interests in both telephonic and oral arbitration hearings. My rates are very modest. (No kidding!)

At this writing, it appears that about 50% of all 'Lemon Law' case hearings are held in the consumer's absence, and are based on the information mailed and/or held over the telephone. I strongly suggest that you attend an 'oral' hearing whenever possible, but as long as you do the proper homework on your case (and study this book) you will no doubt, experience satisfactory results.

CHAPTER SEVEN

The Mediation/Arbitration Process

In this chapter we will explore what to expect at both a mediation meeting as well as an 'oral' arbitration hearing. (*and yes, there will be another test!*)

Mediation:

As applied to the 'Lemon Law,' mediation simply means that one or several informal meetings (or conversations) are arranged between both parties to the dispute, always with a neutral third party (mediator) present. At this meeting, both parties state their position in the case and see if there is any way they can reach an agreement among themselves. The neutral third party (mediator) is there to work with both parties (and keep them from hitting each other—*only kidding!*) and to witness any agreements that may be made. A mediation meeting is very informal and may even be held in a local coffee shop, an office, home, or even in your car! It can also be conducted over the phone as a conference call. *Most* mediation meetings are taped by the mediator. *Most* mediation meetings result in a compromise—you are usually offered something less than you are asking for, and the manufacturer's representative may offer something more than just wanting additional chances to repair your vehicle, again and again.

This is not to say that a mediation meeting is something to be avoided. It can accomplish three things to your benefit:
1. **It may resolve your problem**
2. **It shows that you want the problem resolved**

3. It can give you a valuable insight to the car makers viewpoint on this issue—which can be important, if you structure a case for arbitration.

Arbitration:

The dispute resolution process using arbitration, is made available to you at no cost, and is a viable alternative to litigation. While arbitration is considered an informal hearing process, arbitration decisions are legally binding, if the consumer chooses to accept the decision. In the state of California (and most states) the manufacturer is committed to binding arbitration, while the consumer has the option to take it or leave it.

The following list of questions and answers will recap the basics of arbitration:

Q: Do I need an attorney for arbitration?

A: Arbitration is designed as an informal process and can be effectively handled without legal assistance.

Q: Is arbitration binding?

A: Under most state laws the arbitrator's decision is binding on the manufacturer but not on the consumer until it is accepted.

Q: What does arbitration cost?

A: There is no cost to the consumer for the dispute resolution process or the arbitration hearing. The consumer is only obligated to pay for any legal, technical or expert witness fees that they may incur.

Q: How long does it take for a case decision?

A: Arbitration program guidelines call for quick rsults: the entire process from filing, mediation, an oral, telephonic or written hearing, the decision-making process, and consumer notification of the findings should take less than 60 days!

Q: Can I use the vehicle during the arbitration process?

A: You have every right to continue to drive your vehicle throughout the arbitration process until it is actually repurchased or replaced by the manufacturer. You cannot abuse the vehicle however, and any excessive wear or damage may be deducted from your settlement.

Q: If I am awarded a refund how long will it take to get the money?

A: The law states that the manufacturer has 30 days from the time of the decision to comply.

Q: Must I accept the arbitration decision?

A: Under the California law for example, you are not bound to accept the decision unless you agree to it. In the event a decision is rendered that you find unacceptable, the manufacturer is also released from its obligation to abide by the decision. In other words, you can't say that you don't accept the decision, then later change your mind. Once you say "no" to the decision, you've effectively released the manufacturer from his obligation to honor it.

Q: What can I do if I feel the hearing was unfair?

A: If you feel that you were not given a fair hearing you should report your grievance to the Department of Consumer Affairs in your state.

Q: What can I do if I refuse the arbitration decision"
A: If you decide not to accept the decision from the arbitrator or arbitration panel hearing your case, you can opt to file a civil action against the manufacturer in a court of law, or in some cases, small- claims court. You may wish to consult with an attorney to explore these possibilities. As earlier stated however, if you decide to file a civil case, the fact that you turned down the arbitration decision may be used as evidence against you.

Scheduling Your Hearing Date:

If you have an option to select an oral hearing, I suggest that you do so. In my opinion, an oral (in -person) hearing in front of a single arbitrator hearing your case is the best chance that you, the consumer, has of winning the case! Not all arbitration programs however, offer the consumer the option of an oral, in -person hearing.

If you are scheduled to attend an oral hearing, here are a few tips: Most hearings are set for weekdays between normal hours of 9:00AM –5:00PM.
Most arbitration hearings take between one and two hours. You should schedule your day to be at least an hour early for your hearing. What you **never** want to do is to show up late!!!

Attire:

While your hearing is informal, it is still considered a business function and is generally within a business environment.

While there is no mandatory dress code, business-like attire is strongly suggested. A suit and tie is appropriate if possible, or if you don't have time to go home and change, you can always bring a clean shirt with you and change in the restroom. The best choice is to bring your "hearing" clothes to the job and change before you leave for the hearing. Remember, *look* confident –*be* confident!

Before we proceed to the details of what happens in an oral hearing, I again want to stress the importance of properly completing the forms and understanding other important data for your case. *(And yes, another test!)*

The Arbitration Agreement Form:

The single most important document relating to both the outcome of your case and the award that you receive is the Agreement to Arbitrate Form! Plain and simple! This form in a legal sense, represents your *entire* case—so if you don't list your specific problems and expected remedies, chances are you won't get them! If there is one legal loophole that can severely damage a consumer's case, it would be underrating this all-important form! As discussed earlier in the book, most faulty decisions and poor award judgments can be traced to the data submitted (or omitted) from this form. If you are sent an "Application" form or "Customer Claim Form" - treat them all like they were the powerful Agreement form– because they probably are!

There are two main elements of the legal "Agreement" form that if found in a simple "application" or "customer claim form," are a dead giveaway that it is really 'a wolf in sheep's clothing' and you'd better be careful. Anything that smacks of "Nature of Dispute" or "Decisions Sought" areas of the legal dispute application, no matter how innocently worded, may be there to get you to lower your guard. Here are a few examples taken directly from forms that pretend not to be what they are:

"Briefly describe your unresolved service concern(s) be low. Attach legible copies of applicable repair orders, etc. Or this one is a real case killer. . ."*Brief description of the problem."*

As you can see, both actual examples are really asking the all important Nature of Dispute. While the *"briefly describe"* . . .instruction may sound innocuous and harmless to most folks, remember what happened in our first case study when the consumer did not specifically ask that her incidental damages be considered *(because she was asked to briefly describe)* on her application (agreement) form and it cost her $2,000!

Then we have veiled questions like: *"Describe what you want done to resolve your concern"* and *"what resolution are you seeking?"*

Both the above are seeking to fill the "Decisions Sought" element in your case, without of course, telling you about it! Out of the several forms that I had the manufacturers send me, only one appeared to be somewhat "official" in as much as it had three carbon copy pages. The others were simply a single sheet of paper. None of them stated their importance to the case, or asked you to be precise with answers!

Your case may be heard and your award made, based only on the information given on this form!!

Even if the arbitrator wanted to give you a fair and just award, he may not be allowed to *if you didn't list your case properly or omitted critical information to start with!* A case hearing is restricted to considering the elements listed in **Nature of Dispute** and the award decisions are only based on what was requested within the **Decisions Sought** element of your case filing papers. You can't add things on the day of your hearing.

So, when the car maker sends you a simple "Customer Claim Form" and under the section asking you to "describe what you want" to resolve the problem, you will know better than to ask them to "buy back your vehicle at the purchase price" . . .because that, minus the discounted value of use, is *all* you will get!

Would car makers really, really take advantage of me like that?

Let's answer that question this way . . . If you had one thousand faulty cars that you knew you had to buy back from the public, but could save your company and your shareholders $6,000 on each one just by making a "form" much simpler for the public to complete, (and hiding a few facts) do you think the **six million dollars** savings would be worth it??

Completing The Form:

Yes, yes, I *know* we covered many aspects of the importance of the Agreement to Arbitrate Form (and it's many aka's (also known as) in past chapters but I am going to cover it again, in *detail!* Your entire case may depend on it! When you consider that nearly 50% of all resolution program awards (or lack of) are made *only* on the contents of the document, you must realize it is the most important paper relating to your case. Again, if what appears to be a simple "application" form is sent to you from the car maker, you should complete it as if it were the all-important Agreement to Arbitrate! If there is no room on the form for the necessary details of your case (there seldom is). . . attach another page to it.

Nature of Dispute:

In the *"tell us what the problem seems to be"* section of the form is where you list the exact problem or problems that led you to file your claim. If your Turbo Toad is overheating at freeway speeds, hard starting in the morning, makes knocking or rattling noises when you step on the gas and puffs green smoke at stop lights . . . You must list all of this!

Nobody expects you to be an engineer or to use automotive terms or to even venture a guess at what the problem is; all that is required is that you list what the problem sounds like, feels like, smells like, or looks like, as descriptively as you can. If you have had transmission problems when the car wouldn't shift into forward or reverse within the last six months, say so. Explain these events, where they happened, and even the time of day, if you can remember it. In most cases, the only information the arbitrator will have is what you *descriptively* tell them on the form, your repair order (RO'S) copies and what the manufacturer tells them on *their* form! If you just reference your comments to the failed repair order copies that you have attached, the arbitrators may think that the problem isn't serious enough for you to mention the details.

While you probably told the service manager and the dealer and the factory rep several times about your list of defects, and you feel that everybody in the state knows the problems you're having . . . you should know that the arbitrator is not allowed to see, or take into consideration, outside evidence to your case that is not listed on the form! On the other hand, *do not water-down your case by giving information about unrelated repairs and incidental problems not directly related to the main reasons you are making your claim!*

In the event your claim is for a "Monday" vehicle that has been out of service and in the repair shop for more than a total of 30 days for a number of problems, then you should list *each* problem specifically: "January 9th the passenger door fell off. February 12th drivers-side headlight fell out and the power seat wouldn't move, etc., etc.,"

Do not use catch-all phrases like: *"including, but not limited to"* when describing vehicle problems. Making statements like: *"excessive engine noise and other related problems"* are too general and will not be admissible for consideration! You must take the time to be specific. Now let's look at a few good and bad examples:

A Good Example:

The Consumer states that she has had continuing problems since delivery of her Super Neptune XR-2B coupe due to vehicle defects: rough engine idle, engine 'knocking' noises at all speeds, excessive brake squealing noise and a grinding noise when stopping, 'clunking' noises in the steering wheel when turning right and her air conditioner will only blow warm air. She has had the vehicle in for repair six times in three months and the problems still continue.

In the above example, all the listed problems would, in my opinion, qualify for a vehicle buy-back (with the exception of the air conditioner) because she has exceeded the number of repair attempts, with no results—and the problems affect the use and safety of the vehicle.

Bad Example:

Customer contends that there are many problems with her Astro Turf Special sedan, including but not limited to: engine, transmission, paint and sun roof operation.

Remember, your case depends on the evidence that you have and the testimony that you make (oral or written) but can only be heard based on the problems that you specifically list on the Agreement to Arbitrate Form!

Decision Sought:

If any part of the form letter asks *"describe what you want done"* it is looking to satisfy the Decision Sought requirement found on all Agreement to Arbitrate Forms. This is the area to put into practice all the math you learned throughout the book.

Here is a right and wrong example to help you on your way.

Bad Response:

Under "Decisions Sought" (on the form) the consumer that didn't find time to read this book has written:

"I would really like Snakebite Motors, USA, to buy back my 'Venom XR-2VM' for the full purchase price of $12,750.10."

Good Response:

Under any area of the form that asks what the consumer would like, we would rather like to find this:

" I respectfully request that LAX Motors, Inc. repurchase my vehicle under the provisions of the state of: (your state) 'Lemon Law' resolution program for the amount of $17,460.00 which is summarized as follows:

    $10,960. Base price
    $ 2,000. Trade-in allowance
    $ 1,000. Factory sun roof
    $ 600. Transportation charges
    $ 873. Sales tax
    $ 357. Registration fees
    $ 165. License fees

$ 100. Smog certificate
$16,055.00 Total cost. **Plus incidental damages of:**

$175. Rental car cost (see enclosed receipts)
$125. Towing costs (see enclosed receipts)
$ 75. Emergency road repair
$780. Extended warranty cost
$250. Loan origination fee

$1,405.00 Total incidental damages

$17,460.00 Total reimbursement sought

Note: Now you and I both know that there is a discounted value of use cost applied to vehicle repurchases, (DVU) and you could indicate that amount if you wish, but I wouldn't do their work for them.

What you have effectively accomplished by submitting a polished and accurate Agreement to Arbitrate Form is a number of positive things:
You clearly indicate that you are not an easy mark and will not roll-over for any offer they present to you.

You have placed the arbitrator or arbitration panel on the defensive. They are now in a position where they must consider the merits of each and every element presented within both the "Nature of Dispute" and "Decisions Sought." A presentation like this makes it very difficult for the arbitrator to dispute any part of your award claim! You have effectively tied the "Nature of Dispute" element directly to the "Decisions Sought" requirement . . . and brought them both to conform to the 'Lemon Law' sections and code carried by your state!

CHAPTER EIGHT

The Arbitration Hearing

Attending an oral arbitration hearing is no reason to panic or suffer undue apprehension. I have attended hundreds . . on both sides of the table. With the "ironclad" case that you have prepared with the help of this book, you should be straining at the leash to get there!

To lessen your anxiety a bit, why don't we walk through a typical oral arbitration hearing, but before we do, let's start at your house on the morning of the arbitration. The kitchen table will do just fine!

Purchase Contract:

Okay . . . we'll need to bring the original purchase contract (or copy) that will show: when, where, from whom and for how much you paid for your vehicle. Got that! . . . Good! Yes, include any trade-in allowance too!

Repair Orders:

Yes, list them in chronological order starting with the first repair attempt. No, we don't need to bring *all* the repair orders, just the ones that have a bearing on your case. Remember, we need four repair attempts on one or two problems . . . or *lots* of repair attempts (the 30 days in the repair shop clause).

Correspondence Files:

Yes, bring any and all letters that you have written regarding the vehicle problems, including any replies. This file is a good place to put any letters from friends, neighbors or co-workers who have experienced any part of the vehicle problem. If you have a letter from an 'expert witness' this file is where it should go as well.

Collateral and Incidental Damages:

Collateral damages are any additional costs that you incurred over the base price that you paid. Trade-in, factory options, taxes, transportation costs, etc.

Incidental damages include costs associated with the problem, not directly attributable to the vehicle such as: rental car costs, towing charges, an extended warranty on the vehicle. If the vehicle is financed, you will want to contact the lender or find the loan agreement to see if there was a 'loan origination fee' or a pre-payment penalty if you pay the balance off early. (You must do this to get a clear title so that you can return the vehicle). Oh, also bring your 'extended warranty' contract that shows the payment amount that was added to your bill.

No, you can't try to get compensated for time from work—neither can you get a refund on the interest rate charged by the lender on the <u>balance</u> of the loan.

Proof of Insurance:

An oral arbitration hearing usually requires that the arbitrators inspect the vehicle and take it for a ride to see if they too can experience the problem. You *must* bring proof of insurance on the vehicle or the arbitrators will not be able to drive or even ride in the vehicle . . . and your case will go directly down the dumper!

Wash and Clean the Car:
Your vehicle will be inspected by the arbitrator or arbitrators hearing your case. The vehicle must show that you have taken good care of it both outside and within. No bags of laundry on the back seat or dirty diapers on the floor! There may be as many as three arbitrators who will want to ride in the vehicle to experience the problem, but not the dog drool on the back seat arm rest! Have the vehicle thoroughly cleaned, both inside and out.
A clean and neat car is a good reflection of how you've maintained it. This can put big points on your side of the psychological bargaining table!

Itemized Summary Sheet:
In the "Decisions Sought" part of the last chapter you completed a comprehensive summary of the award that you expect under the 'Lemon Law.' You certainly want to bring this!

Discounted Value of Use:
Called the DVU or MOF calculation, you should have a separate paper showing your figures and the formula that applies. If you drove your vehicle 3,500 miles before it went in for service for the problem that started it all, and the vehicle now has 8,700 miles, you want to be able to show that you know what you should and shouldn't be charged for.

Make Five Copies:

Make five copies of your entire case and neatly place them in five file folders. You will hand them out at the hearing to the Panel of three arbitrators, the manufacturers rep and you will want to keep a copy for yourself.

The Hearing:

Okay . . . You have your case files and information down pat. The vehicle is scrubbed inside and out and you're wearing your Sunday suit (or clean, pressed clothes). You arrive an hour early . . . now what?

In all likelihood, the hearing will be located in an office building and you will find yourself in the reception area, probably looking directly at the manufacturers representative sitting across from you. *Smile and be nice!*

When your case is called, you will be led into a conference room by the Case Administrator, and you will be introduced to the arbitrator or the panel members. You will then be asked to have a seat and the arbitrator or Panel Chairperson will explain the general hearing procedure and read aloud the agreement to arbitrate that you have filled-out and ask you if it is correct. Both parties to the case (and any witnesses or experts that you may have brought) will be sworn-in and asked to sign a copy of the oath. In arbitration hearings, the consumer (plaintiff) is asked to present their side first.

The best place to start is when you first noticed the problem that led to your 'Lemon Law' case. Now would be a good time to hand out the file folders with the copies of your case, to everyone involved. As you explain the problem and the attempts to repair it, you can refer to the repair order numbers or other information, so that the arbitrator and manufacturer's representative can follow the events. It's all very casual, very informal, nobody jumping up shouting *"I object!"* (like on LA Law). Testimony like this, in addition to being easy on your nerves, is also easy for the arbitrator to follow and helps reinforce your case.

No one at the hearing will interrupt you when you are giving your version of the events . . . with the exception of the arbitrator, who may want clarification on something you just said. You will not be cross-examined by anybody: *("did you really hear the transmission fall on the road . . .or did you just THINK you heard the transmission hit the road!)* You should direct all your statements to the arbitrator or panel members.

Your opening statement is really just a conversation with the arbitrator and can go something like this . . . *"After purchasing my Turbo Toad in June, 02 and driving it for three months, I noticed it began shifting funny . . . like it was slipping or something . . . I also noticed a few small puddles of a reddish fluid on my driveway. I took the car in for repair of this problem on September 21st and it is listed on repair order 132-20-085. The car only had 3,000 miles on it at the time. The dealer kept the car for three days. When I got the car back, the problem and fluid leaking started again the next morning . . ."*

You are allowed to continue with your statement until you are satisfied that you have covered all the items necessary to make your case. You should keep in mind a key requirement of the 'Lemon Law,' that the problem or problems you are having with the vehicle clearly affect the "value, use or safety of the vehicle."

After you have completed your testimony, the manufacturer's representative will be given the opportunity to speak as well and explain what has been done to try to solve the problem. It is usually quite brief.
At this point in the hearing, the vehicle will be inspected— and most likely driven.

During the vehicle inspection the arbitrator will examine the overall condition of the vehicle, verify the VIN identification number and check the mileage. If the problem is one that could be experienced with a test drive, the arbitrator will ask both you and the auto representative to go along. If the vehicle can only accommodate two people, the arbitrator will test the vehicle alone (the arbitrator may not be alone with either party for any reason whatsoever).

If you feel that you could repro-duce the noise or other problematic elements of the vehicle, you may suggest that you drive the car.

On completion of the vehicle inspection phase, everyone will return to the hearing room, and you will again be asked if there is anything you would like to add to the testimony before the hearing is officially closed. If you feel that you have the orator qualities of Clarence Darrow, you may want to make a closing statement, such as:

"I would like to thank you for the opportunity to state my case under the 'Lemon Law'. In the event that it is your decision to award the repurchase of this vehicle, I have sub-mitted what I feel, is a fair repurchase claim under the law. This amount includes both collateral and incidental dam-ages that I have incurred during this period. Thank you again, for your time and considerations."

After all closing testimony has been made, the arbitrator will call the hearing to a close and state that a decision will be made and submitted to both parties within ten working days.

The total time for the hearing and vehicle inspection will range between one and two hours.

CHAPTER NINE

The Lemon Law Decision

There are basically three decisions that the arbitrator or arbitration panel can make in your case:

1. A decision in your favor
2. A decision against you
3. An interim decision

In all three of the above scenarios, you will be notified of the decision, and the 'reasons for decision' by mail, usually within two weeks from the hearing date. Let's review a sample of all three as well as the reasons that motivated the arbitrator to make it. (It's always good to know such things).

Favorable:

Ed Sell Motors, Inc. shall repurchase Mr. Smith's 1999 Wombat Special for the amount of: $14,360.20, within 30 days of the date of their acceptance. At the time of the transaction, Mr. Smith shall deliver the vehicle in similar condition to that inspected and with clear title. Ed Sell Motors is hereby directed to contact Mr. Smith to arrange the transaction at a mutually agreeable time and location.

Favorable Reasons:

(Listed in the decisions letter) While Ed Sell Motors, Inc. effected repairs to the vehicle in a noteworthy manner, we find that the problems have not been resolved . We therefore conclude that after one year of repair attempts, the vehicle cannot be repaired to normal operating conditions in order to meet the stated warranty guidelines of this vehicle.

We also concur with the figures submitted by Mr. Smith, which include both collateral and incidental damages and costs, having amended this amount by the Discounted Value of Use calculation of: $425.00 for vehicle use prior to problem documentation.

Unfavorable Decision:

Repurchase of this vehicle is denied.

Unfavorable Reasons:

During the test drive of the vehicle, some slight noise in the power steering unit was detected as well as a slight steering wheel vibration, that in our opinion, are considered 'normal' for this type and make of vehicle. It is additionally our opinion that neither constitutes a safety hazard (as claimed by the consumer) to the normal operation of this vehicle.

Interim Decision:

A third decision in a 'Lemon Law' case is an 'Interim Decision,' which is occasionally awarded when both sides present an equally strong case to the arbitrator, or the arbitrator isn't totally convinced that the problem is not repairable.

An interim decision is always conditional, as it gives the manufacturer a final opportunity to fix the problem within a specified time period (usually 30 days). If after the final repair attempt the consumer is still displeased, the consumer is allowed to file for a case settlement hearing based on the case records on file. If the consumer *does not* contact the hearing offices within the allocated time, the arbitrator will assume the repairs were effective and close the case.

Interim Decision Sample:

LAX Motors shall effect repair to Mr. Smith's 2002 'Grand Toad II' as follows:
The transmission of this vehicle shall be replaced with a new transmission for this make and model vehicle.
Within 30 days of the customers acceptance, LAX Motors shall complete the above directed repairs. If the customer does not contact this office within 45 days of the completion of repairs, it will be assumed that the repairs are satisfactory and this decision will then become final.

SUMMARY:

The consumer laws, civil codes, arbitration programs and procedures described in this book represent many years of concentrated efforts by federal and state agencies and consumer groups to provide a fair consumer relief system. While not perfect by any means, this state and other state guided 'Lemon Laws' continue to serve us all very well. On a national level, thousands of 'Lemon Law' cases are heard each year.

Consultancy:

If you feel you need help preparing your 'Lemon Law' case and may want my opinion, my fee is $100. per hour with a half-hour minimum charge ($50.) plus expenses. Initial contact is best made at the website listed below or my special publisher e-mail address: hoppyccn@aol.com

Please feel free to write me if you think you have a problem that is not covered in this book or related questions. You can also contact me at: **lemonlawgoessour.com**

Joseph J. Caro c/o
CCN Publishing
P.O. Box 7486
Long Beach, CA 90807

The following pages will overview the specific 'Lemon Law' statutes of your state as applied to qualifications, awards and procedures in force during the writing of this book. As laws may change in a short course of time, you should contact the Department of Consumer Affairs in your state for any updates. The following are not complete legal statutes and have been edited for informational content.

State of California
Lemon Law Overview

Summary:
Applies to passenger vehicles purchased, leased, transferred or registered in California excluding motorcycles and off-road vehicles. **Presumption Policy:** 18 months or 18,000 miles, whichever occurs first.

Repair Attempts: four repair attempts, 30 calendar days out of service, or two repair attempts for a substantial defect that may cause death or serious injury.

"Consumer" means the purchaser, lessee or transferee, for other than for purposes of resale of a motor vehicle which is used primarily for personal, family or household purposes and any other person entitled by the terms of the manufacturer's warranty to enforce the obligations of such warranty. The law also applies to a new motor vehicle with a gross vehicle weight under 10,000 pounds that is bought or used primarily for business purposes by a person, including a partnership, limited liability company, corporation, association, or any other legal entity, to which not more than five motor vehicles are registered in this state.

"Motor Vehicle" means a motor vehicle excluding motorcycles and off-road vehicles which was subject to a manufacturer's express warranty at the time of original delivery. This term not only includes new motor vehicles but also demonstrators; the chassis, chassis cab, and propulsion system of a new motor home; and any other motor vehicle sold with a manufacturer's new car warranty.

"Manufacturer's Express Warranty" means the written warranty, so labeled, of the manufacturer of a new motor vehicle, including any terms or conditions precedent to the enforcement of obligations under the warranty.

"Mileage Deduction Formula" The lessee or the buyer may be charged for the use of the vehicle regardless of whether the vehicle is replaced or the purchase price is refunded. The amount that may be charged for use is determined by multiplying the actual price of the new vehicle by a fraction having as its denominator 120,000 and as its numerator the number of miles traveled by the vehicle before it was first brought in for correction of the problem. For example: if the car had traveled 6000 miles before it was first brought in for correction of the problem, the lessee or buyer could be charged 5% (6,000/120,000=5%) of the purchase price for usage.

Law Application: The law applies for the entire period of your warranty. For Example: if your vehicle is covered by a three year warranty and you discover a defect after two years, the manufacturer will have to replace the vehicle or reimburse you as outlined above if the manufacturer or its representative is unable to conform the vehicle to the express warranty after a reasonable number of attempts to do so.

Presumption Statutes: A special provision often called the 'Lemon Law', helps determine what is a reasonable number of attempts for problems that substantially impair the use, value, or safety of the vehicle. The 'Lemon Law' applies to these problems if they arise during the first 18 months after the consumer receives delivery of the vehicle or within the first 18,000 miles on the odometer, whichever occurs first. During the first 18 months or 18,000 miles, the 'Lemon Law' presumes that a manufacturer has had a reasonable number of attempts to repair the vehicle if either (1) the same problem results in a condition that is likely to cause death or serious bodily injury if the vehicle is driven and the problem has been subject to repair two or more times by the manufacturer or its agents, and the buyer or lessee has at least once directly notified the manufacturer of the need for the repair of the problem as provided in the warranty or owner's manual or (2)

The same problem has been subject to repair four or more times by the manufacturer or its agents and the buyer has at least once directly notified the manufacturer of the need for the repair of the problem as provided in the warranty or owner's manual or (3) The vehicle is out of service because of the repair of any number of problems by the manufacturer or its agents for a cumulative total of more than 30 days since delivery of the vehicle.

In California, the Lemon Law presumption is a guide and not an absolute rule. A judge or arbitrator can assume that the manufacturer has had a reasonable number of chances to repair the vehicle if all of the conditions are met. The manufacturer however, has the right to try to prove that it should have the chance to attempt additional repairs, and the consumer has the right to show that fewer repair attempts are reasonable under the circumstances.

If the manufacturer maintains a state certified arbitration program, the consumer must submit the warranty dispute to the arbitration program before the consumer can take advantage of the presumption in court. Arbitration is an alternative to court proceedings. The consumer may assert the presumption during arbitration. Information about any arbitration should be described in the warranty or owner's manual.

Not every manufacturer maintains a state certified program in California. You should check with the Department of Consumer Affairs Arbitration Certification Program at: **1-800-952-5210**.

California does have special provisions for vehicles that are not "new." There are many general rules that apply for vehicles (motorcycles included) that are sold with an express written warranty (living quarters of mobile homes as well) and "used" vehicles sold with an express written warranty.

You should contact the California Department of Consumer Affairs for details.

The Song-Beverly Warranty Act does not apply if the problem was caused by abuse of the vehicle after the vehicle was delivered.

There is a four year statute of limitations in California to bring a law suit for breach of warranty or for violations of Song-Beverly. You should act promptly to try to resolve the problem fairly and quickly without legal action if possible.

NOTES

NOTES

NOTES

Made in United States
Orlando, FL
05 November 2023

Maybe the woman was dead. Kenzie said the woman had been strangled.

Still, this felt too surreal. He needed to examine every angle.

He reached the wooden walkway bordering the water and paused.

It almost seemed like no one was out here. But that couldn't be true. Not based on what Kenzie had seen.

If a woman had gone into the water . . . that meant her killer had to be close by.

His muscles bristled as he glanced around again.

Was someone watching him?

He wasn't sure. But he couldn't just stand here.

Instead, he paced the dock, looking for signs that something had happened.

But this harbor felt like a ghost town.

Not like the scene of a crime.

However, if what Kenzie said was accurate and someone had been strangled and pushed into the water, Jimmy James needed to find her and help her.

Unless it was too late.

He rushed back to the marina office.

If he was going to find the woman in time, he was going to need Kenzie's help. Otherwise, this felt like a wild goose chase.

CHAPTER TWO

"TELL me again exactly what you saw." Police Chief Cassidy Chambers stood in front of Kenzie and Jimmy James at the harbor, not far from the boat Kenzie had seen the woman pushed from.

The darkness continued to deepen around them, only offset by the glow of the headlights from the chief's SUV and the beam of two flashlights carried by her officers as they searched the area.

Kenzie shivered and repeated her story . . . again.

As she finished, she rubbed her temples, feeling the start of a headache coming on.

What a nightmare.

She thought things would get back to normal after the chaos of her first charter. But that clearly wasn't true. There was still more turmoil in her future.

Chief Chambers turned her gaze on Jimmy James. "By the time you got out here, you didn't see anything? There were no signs of this woman?"

Jimmy James shook his head, a grim expression on his face. "Unfortunately, no. It was probably less than five minutes from the time I heard Kenzie scream until I reached the water by the yacht. But there were no signs of movement anywhere."

"The man who did this obviously ran and hid." It was the only thing that made sense to Kenzie.

Actually, none of this made sense.

The woman's body should be floating in the water. The man should have run to evade capture. There should be some kind of evidence somewhere.

But there was none.

Chief Chambers lowered her notepad and focused her gaze on Kenzie. Her tone was soft as she said, "I'm not saying I don't believe you, Kenzie. I'm just trying to collect all the facts. My officers are searching the docks for any evidence."

"Can't you search that man's boat? Maybe there's evidence there." Kenzie nodded at the yacht where the incident had occurred. The boat's name was *Seas the Day*, and, if she had to guess, it was probably fifty-five feet, with a sleek design.

"We're waiting for our search warrant first," the chief explained. "Sometimes, these things take time. But we're working on it."

Kenzie nodded, although she didn't feel certain about anything. She knew what she'd seen. That man had strangled the woman and then pushed her from the top deck of the boat.

Every time Kenzie closed her eyes, the images replayed there.

Jimmy James put his arm around her shoulders, pulled her close, and murmured, "It's going to be okay."

She nodded, unable to shake the shock still coursing through her. Shock mixed with anger at what the man had done, what he might get away with. The combination of emotions felt toxic.

Chief Chambers turned to Jimmy James. "Do you have a list in the office of who's renting this boat slip?" She nodded toward *Seas the Day*.

He nodded. "Stevie-o has it in there somewhere. I'm sure I can find it."

Stevie-o was Jimmy James' friend and the harbormaster here.

"Would you do me a favor? Maybe we can speed up this process if you go find out who the owner of that yacht is. We can give him a call, and maybe he'll let us onboard of his own free will."

"Shouldn't he be onboard now?" Kenzie stared at the yacht and felt her jaw tighten. "If you own a yacht like that, you don't usually get a hotel to stay in overnight."

"That's a good point." Chief Chambers frowned and followed Kenzie's gaze. "But until we know more answers, let's try not to jump to any conclusions."

Kenzie nodded. The chief's words made sense.

Her emotions were tangling with her logic, and she needed to get a grip.

Chief Chambers would figure out some answers. She and her officers just needed a little more time.

———

JIMMY JAMES WATCHED as a Mercedes pulled into the parking lot fifteen minutes later. A man climbed out and marched toward them. Based on the expensive polo shirt and khakis this guy wore, Jimmy James could only assume this was the owner of *Seas the Day*.

Even though it was almost midnight, it didn't appear the man had been asleep. His hair was still in place, and his clothes didn't look rumpled.

The man paused in front of Chief Chambers, his narrowed eyes almost appearing to scowl. "What's going on? Something happened with my boat?"

"Thank you for coming." Chief Chambers snapped her head straighter as she observed the man. "Are you Thatcher Davenport?"

"I am. Now, what's this about?" His voice sounded brisk and impatient.

Irritation flickered through the chief's gaze, but she remained even-keeled. "Someone reported seeing a woman assaulted and shoved off your boat into the water tonight."

He scoffed and jerked his head back as if that news shocked him. "That's impossible. I haven't been here all evening, and the boat is locked up."

Jimmy James stood beside Kenzie, watching and listening to the entire interaction. He tried not to form too many judgments, but this man was clearly so pompous that it was hard not to.

"If you don't mind me asking, where have you been?" Chief Chambers stared at Thatcher, her gaze unwavering.

"I was having dinner with some friends who are staying on the island for the week, and they invited me to stay over at their beach house tonight so we could catch up. We've been shooting the breeze for most of the evening. Why?"

"It's just a routine question," Chief Chambers assured him. "I would like to board your boat to look around and make sure that everything is okay."

Thatcher stiffened as he seemed to consider the implications of her request. But, finally, he nodded. "Of course. Whatever you need to do. But I person- ally think this whole thing is ridiculous. I have ten people who can verify I was with them this evening."

"And I will need their names. But remember that

someone could have snuck aboard your boat. Do you have anyone manning it when you're not there?"

He scowled again. "I do, but I gave them the night off. Thought this area was safe. Thought there were people around to keep an eye on things."

His cool gaze went to Jimmy James, and his look turned pointed.

This man was sizing him up, trying to figure out if Jimmy James was one of those dockworkers who'd failed to keep the area secure.

His dislike of the yacht owner grew stronger.

"How long are you here?" Chief Chambers continued.

"I planned on staying until the end of the week so I could visit with my friends more before getting back to my summer home in Florida. It's a little too hot down there at this time of year, even for my tastes."

Chief Chambers nodded slowly. "Understandable. I'm going to go look on your boat myself, and if you would please stay with my officer, he has some additional information he needs to get from you."

"Whatever you need." The man's words came out briskly, as his jaw seemed to lock in place in annoyance. "Here are the keys."

As Chief Chambers walked toward the gangplank and an officer walked away with Thatcher,

Jimmy James turned to Kenzie. She was obviously shaken, and he was concerned about her.

"How are you holding up?"

She shrugged and shook her head then shrugged again. "I don't even know how I'm doing. This all just seems like a nightmare."

Jimmy James wrapped his arms around her and pulled her close. As he did, Kenzie nestled her head against his chest. The way she so easily molded against him made Jimmy James feel like a million bucks. If he could hold her like this for the rest of his life, he would be a happy man.

"I know it seems like a nightmare," he said. "But hopefully Chief Chambers will find something on that boat. Maybe we'll have some answers soon."

Kenzie pulled away, and her gaze trailed across the lot to Thatcher Davenport. "He looks like someone who would get along well with my father and Leesa."

Leesa was Kenzie's stepmom, and, from what Jimmy James had heard, she was the type who liked to keep up appearances. He knew the two of them had a strained relationship and that Kenzie didn't think highly of her stepmom.

Jimmy James followed her gaze and frowned as he watched Thatcher talking to Officer Dillinger. The man's motions appeared stiff.

"What do you think that guy does for a living?" Kenzie asked.

Jimmy James shrugged as he studied the man. "He either owns his own business or he's a lawyer. What do you think?"

"I'm leaning toward lawyer. He gives off that vibe somehow."

Those were Jimmy James' thoughts exactly. Thatcher Davenport seemed like an ambulance chaser disguised as someone too prestigious to accept that label. He probably took on big cases that made him lots of money. Money that allowed him to buy a yacht like the one in front of them.

Jimmy James wasn't envious of rich people, but he didn't like how they often acted pompous and above others.

He stared at *Seas the Day* another moment.

He couldn't stop picturing a woman being choked and then pushed into the water.

If he'd just gotten out here more quickly . . . if he'd looked more fervently . . . would he have been able to save her?

However, a body hadn't been discovered yet, which still seemed strange to him. Something wasn't adding up.

Several minutes later, Chief Chambers strode from the boat toward Thatcher, handed him his keys, and quietly spoke with him. The man nodded, not seeming overly upset by whatever she said.

Kenzie straightened as she stared at the scene. Her eyes narrowed with thought. "What do you think she's telling him?"

"That she likes his shirt?"

Kenzie playfully elbowed him. "Good one."

"Just trying to lighten the mood."

After chatting with Thatcher for several minutes, Chief Chambers nodded toward the man and stepped back.

She glanced over at Jimmy James and Kenzie and started their way. Based on her frown, she didn't have good news.

Chief Chambers paused in front of them and grimaced. "I'm afraid the boat is as clean as a whistle. My guys searched the water from the docks, and the marine police will be arriving in their patrol boats soon to search as well. But, so far, there's no sign anything happened on Mr. Davenport's boat. I'm not sure whether to say I'm sorry or to celebrate."

"But I *know* what I saw." Kenzie's voice cracked as she said the words.

Chief Chambers pressed her lips together again before saying, "I'm not questioning what you think you saw. But are you sure your eyes weren't deceiving you? It was awfully dark out here."

Kenzie adamantly shook her head, leaving no

room for doubt about how she felt. "I definitely saw a woman being pushed."

Chief Chambers' gaze met Jimmy James', and he saw her unspoken words.

She was afraid Kenzie might be losing her mind, wasn't she?

Jimmy James didn't believe that. But he also had no idea how to explain what had happened tonight.

No evidence. No body.

No crime?

CHAPTER THREE

KENZIE BIT DOWN as Chief Chambers went to join her officers on the other side of the harbor.

She still couldn't believe this was happening. How could that woman's body have disappeared? It made no sense.

She shivered, and it wasn't because of the balmy breeze that swept up from the water.

She had to give credit to the Lantern Beach PD. They *were* swarming the area. Police lights flooded the scene. In the distance, she even spotted a marine police vessel puttering around in the water.

As they stood there on the once-peaceful dock, Jimmy James' hands went to her shoulders. He gently massaged her tight muscles, working out the knots that had formed.

"Maybe when it's daylight outside, the police will

discover something they didn't see before," Jimmy James murmured.

Kenzie wished those words brought her comfort, but they didn't. She was still on edge. The woman who'd fallen into the water couldn't have just disappeared.

But without a body, Kenzie couldn't blame everyone for the strange looks they gave her.

Certainly, there *had* to be some kind of evidence . . .

Yet she'd seen Thatcher drive up. He wouldn't have had time earlier to get his car and pull away while she and Jimmy James were outside watching. And she hadn't seen anyone else on that boat . . .

"Does he look like the man you saw?" Jimmy James nodded toward Thatcher as he stood near the cops in the distance. Thatcher's hands were on his hips, and his stance looked tense and bristled as he stared at his boat. "Could he match the basic description?"

Jimmy James still stood behind her, his hands on her shoulders, and Kenzie leaned back against him, relishing his strength and support.

She followed his gaze to Thatcher and let out a sigh. "It's hard to say. I only saw silhouettes. He *could* be the same size as the man but . . . I just can't say for sure."

As if Thatcher heard them, he turned their way and started toward them.

Kenzie braced herself for whatever this conversation would hold. Based on the squared set of Thatcher's shoulders and his determined stride, he was going to give them the third degree.

He stopped in front of them, and his hands went to his hips. "Are you the ones who reported this incident?"

Kenzie squeezed her lips together, the man's tone rubbing her the wrong way. Before she could answer, Jimmy James pushed himself in front of her, his muscles bristled with protectiveness.

"Why does it matter?" Jimmy James demanded.

"I have a feeling I know what's going on here." Thatcher's jaw flexed as he stared at them with a judgmental gaze.

Kenzie shook her head, totally clueless as to what he was talking about. "What would that be?"

His gaze narrowed. "You're working for Williams, aren't you?"

Williams? Was she supposed to recognize that name? "I have no idea who Williams is."

Thatcher shifted, irritation rising from him like fog on the water. "Luke Williams? The senator?"

"Why in the world would you think I'm working for him?" Kenzie's voice rose in pitch as she asked the question.

Thatcher stepped closer but quickly backed off as Jimmy James blocked him. He may not have growled, but he might as well have.

But Jimmy James' actions only deterred Thatcher for a moment. He turned back to Kenzie and shook his head. "If this is some kind of scheme, know that I can ruin you."

Kenzie gasped at his sharp tone. As the meaning of his words hit her, she drew back.

Before she could speak, Jimmy James spoke for her. "Is that a threat?"

"It's not a threat. It's reality. You're not going to play these games and think you can get away with them. And I'm not going to let your little bodyguard here scare me either." He looked Jimmy James up and down. "You're just trouble, aren't you?"

As she felt Jimmy James bristle again, Kenzie touched his arm, trying to bring him back to reality.

Jimmy James let out a little growl—a real one, this time—but said nothing. But Kenzie didn't miss how his hands fisted at his side.

"I think you need to leave," Jimmy James hissed.

"Fine." Thatcher took a step back. "But I'll be keeping my eyes on you two. No one is going to play me for a fool. No one."

JIMMY JAMES FELT adrenaline surging through him. Who did that guy think he was? Coming here and threatening them like this? He had another thing coming for him if he thought—

"It's okay, Jimmy James." Kenzie's soft voice pulled him from his thoughts.

He snapped out of his daze and turned to her, studying her expression and anxious to see how she was handling that confrontation. She seemed surprisingly calm as her head tipped back and she let out a breath.

She had so much grace for others. While others might have written certain people off, she seemed to want to dig deeper into their makeup until she learned the truth about them.

Maybe that was why she hadn't run away from him yet.

Most women like Kenzie would.

Jimmy James felt his jaw twitch. "He has no right to talk to you like that."

She shrugged. "Look, I think that the guy is a jerk. I've been around people like him my whole life. And if there's one thing I've learned is that you can't play into him."

Jimmy James watched Thatcher as he climbed into his car. "Could he be the guy behind this?"

She nibbled on her lip for a moment before saying, "I just don't know how he would have gone from strangling a woman and pushing her into the water to driving up in his car fifteen minutes later."

"What about this Luke Williams guy? Do you know anything about him?"

Kenzie shook her head. "No, I don't. Although I think I heard his name on some type of TV ad." Kenzie let out another long breath. "So, why would working for Senator Williams have anything to do with what happened tonight? How were we trying to set someone up?"

"I'm not sure." Jimmy James shrugged, trying to make sense of it himself. "I heard from some guys on a fishing charter that the upcoming race for senate is pretty contentious this year."

"Who is this Williams guy running against?" Kenzie asked. "Do you know? Since I'm not from the area, I haven't kept up with the politics here."

"It's a newcomer named Abe Sampson, if I remember correctly."

She nodded slowly as if storing his name away. "Thatcher must think we're some kind of political operatives. I wonder what Thatcher's connection is with Abe Sampson."

Jimmy James shrugged. "I'm not sure, but it might be worth looking into."

"I'll mention this connection to Chief Chambers when she gets back tonight. I guess there are some perks to staying at the police chief's house."

Jimmy James nodded and glanced at his watch. It had been a long day and detaining Kenzie here would only keep her on edge. The best thing for Kenzie was to get her out of here.

"Speaking of which, maybe I should take you home," Jimmy James said. "It's getting late."

Kenzie slipped her arm in his and nodded. "That sounds like a good idea. Maybe I'll wake up in the morning and discover this was all a nightmare."

Jimmy James wished that would be the case.

But he had a feeling this was far from over.

As he walked with her to his truck, he heard an engine rev.

He turned just as a dark-colored sedan appeared from seemingly nowhere.

It charged right toward them.

As the headlights blinded them, Jimmy James grabbed Kenzie and threw her out of the way.

He only hoped he wasn't too late.

CHAPTER FOUR

AS KENZIE HIT THE GRAVEL, her heart pounded out of control.

What had just happened?

She looked up in time to see a car pulling away from the harbor, driving entirely too fast.

"Are you okay?" Jimmy James asked, cringing as he sat up beside her.

"Thanks to you, I am. Thank you." She rubbed her elbow, which throbbed. She might have a bruise in the morning, but it could have been much worse. She glanced toward the car again. "Did you happen to get a license plate?"

He shook his head. "There wasn't one."

"Do you think that was purposeful?"

"It is dark out here, but it's hard to say. I'll

mention it to Chief Chambers, just in case. In the meantime, let's get you home."

Fifteen minutes later, Jimmy James walked Kenzie to the front door of the beach house where she was staying.

A burst of warmth filled her chest when she remembered how he'd thrown her out of the way tonight, putting himself in potential danger to protect her.

She enjoyed being around Jimmy James more than she'd ever expected. His company was so pleasant, yet exciting.

And when she wasn't with him . . . she wanted to be.

Jimmy James wasn't her type. If someone had asked her a few weeks ago, she would have said her type was more of the academic sort. But something about Jimmy James absolutely fascinated her.

The man was tall and big, with bulging muscles and tattoos. He had a rough past, but he'd turned his life around—and Kenzie thought that was admirable. Really admirable.

In fact, it was easy to live a good life when you were handed everything. But a lot of people Kenzie had grown up around had even found that difficult.

For someone to go from making bad choices to doing a one-eighty was so much more commendable.

That wasn't to mention the fact that Kenzie found Jimmy James' protectiveness adorable. And comforting. He'd been there for her on more than one occasion and had made it clear that he had her back.

They paused on the deck of the oceanfront home.

Kenzie knew that Cassidy was still at the marina, and Ty—Cassidy's husband—had mentioned earlier that he was doing a training exercise with Blackout this evening. That meant no one was inside other than Kujo, their dog.

She and Jimmy James stood there a minute, the ocean breeze flooding over them and the reassuring scent of saltwater slowing her pulse.

She touched his arm and saw him flinch.

That's when she noticed the cut on his arm.

"You're hurt," she murmured.

He glanced down. "It's nothing."

"That's not nothing. You need to clean that up."

"Really, it's—"

"Come inside a moment and let me help. I insist."

Jimmy James didn't argue as she unlocked the door and slipped inside. Kujo greeted them as they entered.

"You stay with him while I go get the first aid kit," Kenzie murmured.

Jimmy James was still standing near the front door when she returned. She pulled out some gauze and spread some ointment on it before dabbing his cut.

It was probably only three inches long and not too deep. Still, it needed to be treated.

When she finished, she pulled out a bandage and pressed it on the edges of the cut.

"There you go. All better."

Jimmy James' gaze caught with hers. "Thank you."

She felt something pass between them as she looked up, realizing she was probably standing entirely too close.

She couldn't look away from the tenderness in his eyes.

When she'd first met him, Kenzie would have never guessed Jimmy James would be the type to have a tender side. Although he was rough and tough on the outside, he was a teddy bear at heart.

At least, he was when it came to her.

The warmth inside her seemed to spread from her heart all the way to her extremities as she stared at Jimmy James' face. At the stubble on his cheek and chin. At the depth of his gaze. At his crooked, handsome smile.

Spontaneously, she reached up and ran her fingers across his cheek.

He sucked in a breath at her touch, and his gaze captured hers, something unseen seeming to lock them together.

"Thank you for everything tonight," Kenzie whispered, her voice scratchier than she'd anticipated.

"Of course."

They'd been hanging out since their charter ended, and Kenzie had thoroughly enjoyed every moment of their time together.

Jimmy James hadn't tried to make any moves yet, although he had taken her for ice cream and dinner and had shown her around the island. Kenzie had almost expected him to try to take their relationship to the next level, but he hadn't.

Part of her was tired of waiting. The man wasn't shy. So, what was his holdup?

"Jimmy James . . . you're a diamond in the rough," Kenzie said softly. "I just wanted to let you know that."

Part of his lip quirked up in a grin. "Really? I wasn't expecting that. But I'll take it."

"I really mean it." Her throat tightened. "I'm glad God brought you into my life."

His eyes widened as their gazes connected, something unseen linking them together. "Kenzie . . . you represent everything I'm not."

Her breath caught as she wondered where he was going with this. "Like what?"

"Everything good."

She tilted her head. "You don't think you have goodness in you?"

He shrugged. "The goodness I have is like a boat that's been beaten beyond repair."

"Nothing's beyond repair. It just takes time and energy."

He shook his head, a touch of disbelief in his gaze. "You deserve so much better than me. I don't have anything to offer you."

"I didn't ask you to offer me anything."

Another emotion flashed in his gaze. Was that . . . affection? Desire? Both?

His eyes went to her lips.

The next instant, his hand slipped behind her head, and he dipped his until their lips met.

When they did, everything disappeared from around Kenzie as pure bliss filled her veins.

"YOU SHOULD PROBABLY GO," Kenzie murmured several minutes later.

Blood still warmly coursed through her veins, and her lips tingled from their kiss. Despite her statement, she remained in his embrace, relishing the feel of his arms around her.

Jimmy James leaned toward her as if he wanted to kiss her again, but he stopped himself. "Probably a good idea."

"Probably." Her throat felt tight as she said the word—especially since all she craved was to get closer, to feel his lips against hers again.

She'd dated before. But something about that kiss . . . it blew all the others she'd ever received out of the water. Maybe it was because she felt like Jimmy James genuinely cared about her.

He pulled her toward him and planted a long kiss on her forehead before stepping back. With one more wave, he stepped from the cottage.

As Kenzie stepped outside to watch him leave, her heart pounded out of control.

What was she doing?

She hadn't come here looking for romance. But what if romance had found her anyway?

Touching her lips, she grinned.

She liked the thought of that.

When Jimmy James' truck disappeared from sight, Kenzie scanned the beach in the distance, her eyes drawn to the area for some unknown reason.

She shivered.

Why did she feel like she was being watched? It didn't make any sense that someone would have followed her here . . . unless this person had seen her face and knew she'd witnessed a murder that wasn't supposed to happen.

She nearly stumbled into the door behind her.

Scanning the shoreline one more time, she didn't see anybody or anything. Maybe she really *was* being paranoid.

Paranoid or astutely observant? Either way, Kenzie needed to get inside. Needed to be somewhere where she felt less exposed.

If the killer did see her, then she wasn't safe right now.

CHAPTER FIVE

JIMMY JAMES FELT like he was walking on clouds as he headed away from Chief Chambers' house.

As he stared out the windshield, he couldn't stop thinking about Kenzie. About how undeserving he was that someone like her would be interested in someone like him. Was it too good to be true?

He wasn't sure. But there was no way he was going to walk away from an opportunity like this. An opportunity like Kenzie.

She was everything he could ever want and more.

As he continued down the road, doubts tried to claim his thoughts. Doubts about how compatible the two of them would be together in the long run. He pushed his uncertainties away.

Not now. For now, Jimmy James would enjoy this moment.

Instead of heading back to the cottage he called home, he veered to the marina. He'd worked there for so long that the place felt like his domain.

It wasn't.

But Jimmy James had worked as a dockhand for many years as well as a first mate on fishing charters, and he'd done various other tasks as needed. He was Harbormaster Stevie-o's right-hand man. Over the past several months, he'd worked hard to get his captain's license, which had required time away and on the water. He'd done that in the winter months when things were slower here at the harbor.

It was a simple life, but he enjoyed it. However, he did want more for his future. That's why he'd taken the job as captain on the charter Kenzie had worked on. The original captain had been murdered and then the backup captain got the stomach flu.

Plus, Kenzie was going to be onboard, and he'd suspected trouble might follow her.

Even though it was the middle of the night, he parked at the marina and sauntered toward the docks. As he did, he paused near the water and stared at *Seas the Day*. The police had gone and everything seemed quiet.

What exactly had happened tonight? Kenzie was a smart girl. She wasn't the type to give into paranoia or to see things that hadn't happened. She'd been in med school before she came to Lantern Beach, so she was clearly intelligent and level-headed.

So, what happened? Why couldn't the police find any evidence of a crime on this boat?

It didn't make any sense to him.

He stared across the water and saw movement in the distance.

Was that a boat out there without any lights on?

It was too dark outside to say for sure.

His heart pounded faster.

He stepped closer, his eyes latched onto the water.

Someone was definitely out there. It couldn't be the marine police. They would have their lights on.

There might be a simple explanation, like somebody who'd gone flounder fishing in the dark.

Or could this boat have something to do with tonight's events?

It was impossible to say at this point. Jimmy James was tempted to jump on his Bayliner and check it out. But by the time he did that, the boat would be gone.

Either way, his back muscles tightened.

Something was going on here. Jimmy James needed to figure out what.

KENZIE HAD AWOKEN SURPRISINGLY EARLY the next morning. Instead of hopping out of bed, she pulled out her laptop and sat in the bed of her temporary bedroom. She looked up any missing women reports in the area, but there were none.

Next, she moved onto researching Abe Sampson and Senator Luke Williams.

She didn't discover anything about them that particularly surprised her. Sampson owned a real estate empire in the Raleigh area but had been moved to go into politics after he'd grown distrustful of government policies. He had a passionate fan base.

Williams had a long history in politics. He'd started as a lobbyist twenty years ago and had grown into a fixture in the DC area. His wife, Lori, was often in the photos with him, smiling and looking like a beautiful armpiece for the picture-perfect senator. The two looked like they were made for each other.

When that research led nowhere, Kenzie looked for anything she could find about Thatcher Davenport.

The man *was* an attorney. She and Jimmy James had been correct. He had his own law firm, he liked to boat and golf, and he often posted pictures of himself on fancy vacations. He was listed as married, but Kenzie didn't see any pictures of the man's wife.

As Kenzie dug deeper, she found a notation on a political website that Thatcher had donated to Abe Sampson's campaign. Her gut feeling told her he might be personally working for the senate hopeful, but she couldn't find confirmation online.

She stared at the computer screen until her eyes got blurry. Then she showered, got dressed, and wandered into the kitchen. The tantalizing scent of bacon and eggs wafted through the air, and Kujo—a golden retriever—came over with a wagging tail to greet her.

Kenzie rubbed the dog's head, instantly missing her own dog, Milo—a mini-labradoodle.

Ty and Cassidy were making breakfast together, both standing near the stove and talking in low tones. Ty had his arms around Cassidy's waist, and the two of them laughed softly about something.

Kenzie stepped back, suddenly feeling like she was interrupting a moment.

The floor squeaked beneath her feet, and they twirled around. When they spotted her, they parted. But both had grins on their faces.

They made an adorable couple and stirred a longing inside Kenzie. She wanted to share that same connection with someone someday.

Jimmy James?

As she remembered their kiss last night, she fought a grin.

Maybe.

Cassidy's sweatpants and T-shirt showed off her growing belly more than her police uniform did.

Kenzie knew just how excited the two of them were about having a baby. Their due date was only a few months away now.

"Good morning." Ty flipped a piece of bacon. "Don't mind us. Cassidy thinks she knows the secret to making crunchy bacon, but I beg to differ."

Kenzie pointed behind her. "Do you want me to come back later?"

"Don't be silly." Cassidy picked up a glass of orange juice. "Have a seat."

Ty grabbed a mug and filled it with coffee before handing it to Kenzie.

She thanked him and then sat at the kitchen table. Kenzie hadn't seen either of them before she went to bed last night, so she hadn't had any time to chat.

Cassidy—the police chief had told Kenzie to call her that when she wasn't on duty—lowered herself across the table from her. "Jimmy James told me about the car that almost hit you last night."

Kenzie nodded. "Talk about an eventful evening . . ."

"But you're okay?" Cassidy studied her face.

"I'm fine." Kenzie waved a hand in the air.

"I'm glad to hear that."

"I don't suppose there have been any updates?" Hope trailed from Kenzie's voice as she stared at the police chief.

Cassidy frowned and took a sip of her orange juice. "I wish there was something I could tell you. But there's nothing."

A question danced on the tip of Kenzie's tongue. She almost feared asking it, feared the answer. But she couldn't let her worries stop her.

"Do you think I made this up?" She held her breath as she waited for Cassidy's response.

"I definitely believe that you think you saw something. You have a good head on your shoulders."

Kenzie played with the rim of the coffee mug, comforted, she supposed, by the affirmation. "I'm not going to be able to stop thinking about this until I have answers."

"You let us handle it." Cassidy locked gazes with her as if to make it clear she was taking this matter seriously. "We're going to continue looking into this. I'm not going to let it drop yet."

Ty sat down beside Cassidy and handed her a plate.

Kenzie felt better knowing that Cassidy wasn't brushing her off. But she wasn't ready to wrap up this conversation yet. Not until she shared what she'd learned. "Did you realize that Thatcher is affiliated with Abe Sampson?"

Cassidy nodded, no signs of surprise in her gaze. "I did some research last night and discovered that."

Kenzie relayed to Cassidy the conversation Thatcher had with her and Jimmy James, careful to mention how abrasive the man was and his implication that Jimmy James was somehow responsible.

Cassidy picked up a piece of toast and shook her head. "I can't believe the nerve of that guy."

"Jimmy James and I were pretty shocked also."

"I'll keep digging," Cassidy assured her. "You just promise me that you'll stay out of this. If someone was murdered . . . then the person responsible probably won't hesitate to kill again."

Kenzie rubbed the rim of her mug again before nodding. "I'll do my best."

CHAPTER SIX

JIMMY JAMES HAD ONLY GOTTEN a few hours
of shut-eye last night. Thankfully, that was all he
needed. He'd never required a lot of sleep.

He'd gotten back to the marina early this
morning and had already done a sunrise fishing
charter, helping one of his friends who had a twenty-
eight-foot Wellcraft.

As he had been out on the water, he'd kept his
eyes open for anything amiss. But he hadn't seen
anything suspicious.

They returned to the dock at eleven. After he'd
helped the guests disembark to brag to everyone
about their catches, he turned to his friend. Tom
Weathersby was in his forties, though his wrinkles
made him look older, and he was an avid fisherman,

who'd even been featured in *National Geographic* once.

Jimmy James nodded toward *Seas the Day*. The boat floated peacefully in the marina as if it were innocent of any wrongdoing. "Do you know anything about the guy who owns her?"

Tom shrugged as he collected the fishing gear and studied each piece, making sure it would be ready for his next guests. "I've talked to him a couple of times. Don't care to talk to him again."

"I had that impression also." Jimmy James grabbed a water hose so they could spray down the interior of the boat. "You know anything else about him?"

"I heard he was a lawyer. Why are you asking?" Tom paused and stared at Jimmy James, curiosity gleaming in his gaze. "You're not the type who usually takes this much interest in others."

Jimmy James shrugged. "Kenzie thought she saw something happen on his boat last night."

"Kenzie? That the girl I've seen you with?"

"It is."

"You look as if you feel like a million bucks when you're with her."

Jimmy James grinned. "I do."

"Good for you, man. Just remember—bad company corrupts good character. She's going to be in big trouble." Tom let out a loud, belly-deep laugh as if the thought were hilarious before punching Jimmy James' arm.

Jimmy James felt his breath catch. He didn't want to let his friend's words get to him. But was there any truth to them?

He shoved the thought aside for another time. "Could we get back to Thatcher?"

Tom's laughter died, and he continued checking his gear, wisps of laughter popping up every few seconds. "Of course. What did your girl think she saw last night? Illegal fishing or something?"

"I wish it was something as simple as fishing. Truth is, someone may have . . . fallen off the boat."

"Fallen off?" He raised an eyebrow.

Jimmy James shrugged, not wanting to sound too dramatic. "After being strangled."

His friend let out a low whistle. "That's a pretty big accusation."

"It is. The police can't find any evidence of it. But she's sure of what she saw."

Tom shook his head before shrugging and placing his final fishing pole back into the rod rack. "I don't know. That guy seems like someone who'd sue a person up and down without thinking twice of it. But killing them? He doesn't seem like he has it in him. But, again, that's just my opinion."

Jimmy James bit down. He had to admit that his friend's assessment sounded right.

Thatcher probably wasn't the type to murder someone in cold blood.

Then again, maybe the best criminals were the ones people never suspected being capable of violence.

AT LUNCHTIME, Kenzie headed toward the marina.

She made a stop on the way at The Crazy Chefette to pick up some sandwiches. The restaurant featured unique food combinations that drew foodies up and down the East Coast to visit. She got a green goddess sandwich for herself and a classic club for Jimmy James.

Jimmy James didn't know Kenzie was coming, but she knew it was nearing time for his lunch break. She planned to surprise him.

She couldn't stop thinking about their kiss last night. Warmth flooded through her every time she mentally replayed feeling his lips against hers.

Could their kiss have been any better?

She didn't think so. She was excited to see what the future might hold for the two of them.

That afternoon the crew of *Almost Paradise* was

meeting to discuss the upcoming charter and whether it would happen. Eddie had called the meeting since he was the main contact right now with Bill Robertson, the boat's owner.

Mr. Robertson planned to find a new captain before the charter could be confirmed. That was the last Kenzie had heard, at least. But, if that was the case, a lot needed to be done before their charter left tomorrow.

She was thankful she was able to stay at Cassidy and Ty's place in the meantime. Otherwise, most of her paycheck would have been eaten up by paying for housing. Ordinarily, the crew would be able to stay on the boat, but, after the last charter, the yacht had to be inspected and searched.

As she pulled into the harbor, a rush of nerves swept through her. Images of last night's events filled her mind.

A woman had been killed here last night.

She sighed and pushed down the heaviness in her chest before grabbing the paper bag filled with their lunch. She climbed from her car and strolled across the gravel lot toward the docks, scanning everything around her as she walked.

She spotted Jimmy James hosing down a boat at the end of the dock.

She couldn't miss him. He was taller and broader

than most of the other guys here. Even in his dark-blue swim trunks and white marina shirt, he still looked edgy and tough.

A smile lit his face when he looked up and saw her. He muttered something to the guy next to him before starting toward her.

Seeing him caused her heart to both flutter and do flips at the same time.

They met halfway, and Jimmy James flashed a grin as he stepped closer. "I'd say good morning, but I guess it's lunchtime now, isn't it?"

"It is. Did you have a good charter?" She nodded toward the boat she'd seen him come off. Part of her felt like this conversation was entirely too normal. The other part welcomed the routine, the illusion that last night's events hadn't happened.

"The guys caught a few tile fish, five mahis, and eight groupers. Not too shabby." He nodded down the docks to where the men displayed their fish and took pictures of them.

"Good for them." She turned back to Jimmy James and held up the bag in her hands, the aroma of melted cheese and toasted bread floating out. "I was hoping that you might want some lunch."

A knot formed between his eyes. "You brought me lunch?"

She shrugged, suddenly wondering if this had been a bad idea. Was she being presumptuous?

Jumping in too quickly? What if Jimmy James was having second thoughts after their kiss last night?

"I did. I figured you needed to eat."

"Aren't you the sweetest thing ever?" A grin stretched across his face. "As a matter of fact, I'm famished. I'm sure whatever you brought is better than the peanut butter and jelly I packed for myself."

As relief washed through Kenzie, she offered him a soft smile, one that felt almost shy.

Shy? She'd been called a lot of things in life but never shy. What was going on with her?

She shoved the thought aside and said, "Perfect. Anywhere in particular you want to eat?"

He glanced around the marina. "I'd say on my boat, but it's pretty sweltering already today, and the bugs are bad. I'm sure Stevie-o wouldn't mind if we used his office if that would be more comfortable for you . . ."

"I'm okay with the heat. The picnic table over there has some shade. How about eating there?" She pointed to one of two tables that had been set up near the back of the parking area, close to a small patch of trees bordering the other side of the marina.

"Perfect. Can you give me ten minutes, and I'll meet you there? I need to wash up."

"That works."

Kenzie strolled toward the picnic table and set out their sandwiches, chips, and drinks. She perched on the wooden bench and waited. Here in the shade, it felt a good ten degrees cooler.

But Jimmy James was right. The hot day held no breeze, which always brought the bugs out. Kenzie had learned that in the brief time she'd been here on Lantern Beach.

As she waited, she glanced around again.

Her breath caught when she saw Thatcher Davenport pull up in his slick silver Mercedes. He unfolded himself from the driver's seat and headed across the parking lot toward the marina office, walking as if on a mission.

Kenzie continued watching as a gruff-looking man with a scraggly dark beard stepped outside to meet him.

It was Stevie-o. Thatcher said something in low tones to the harbormaster before glancing around. The next instant, Stevie-o motioned for Thatcher to follow him inside.

Kenzie frowned. What was that about?

The interaction could be nothing—simply a business matter since Thatcher *was* docked here at the harbor.

Or it could be *something*.

Kenzie nibbled on her bottom lip as she thought about the possibilities.

She almost wished she'd agreed to eat inside after all. Maybe she would have been privy to more information if she had.

CHAPTER SEVEN

"THIS IS REALLY GOOD." Jimmy James took another bite of his sandwich and swallowed. "Thank you for coming to see me. That's really sweet."

Kenzie's gaze wandered briefly behind him again before jerking back to meet his. Was she looking for someone? Most likely, this had something to do with last night's events.

She plastered on a smile that didn't quite reach her eyes as she turned back to him. "Of course. I wanted to make sure I saw you before things got busy."

He narrowed his eyes, sensing the source of her distraction and cutting to the chase. "You're talking about the charter?"

Kenzie seemed to snap back to the present as she frowned at him, her distraction disappearing for a moment. "I'll find out today if it's still on or not. The crew is supposed to meet here at three o'clock."

Jimmy James wished he could be on that boat with Kenzie again. But she was a grown woman, and he had to trust that she could handle herself.

Despite his reasoning, he still wished he was on that boat with her. Maybe for more than one reason. Maybe simply because he liked being around her.

She pointed to the office in the distance before popping a french fry into her mouth. "Stevie-o . . . is he a pretty nice guy?"

Jimmy James slowed his chewing. "Yeah, he's pretty nice. Rough around the edges at times—not that I have any room to talk."

"Do you think he's pretty honest?" Kenzie glanced up at him, her wide eyes full of curiosity.

Jimmy James tilted his head. "What are you getting at?"

"Nothing really." Kenzie shrugged. "I just saw Stevie-o earlier. He was talking to Thatcher. Whatever they were speaking about seemed hush-hush."

Jimmy James glanced back at the office. "It was probably nothing, just business."

Kenzie nodded quickly—a little too quickly, almost like she was trying to convince herself that was true. "That's what I thought also. There's just something about Thatcher Davenport I don't like."

"I can see that. I asked around about him here at the harbor."

"He's a lawyer," Kenzie quickly said.

Jimmy James raised his eyebrows before grabbing a napkin and wiping his mouth, buying time as he formulated his response. "You've been looking into him too, huh?"

She shrugged again as if her curiosity was casual, but Jimmy James suspected it wasn't. He suspected Kenzie had been doing everything she could behind the scenes to find information. Unanswered questions had a way of haunting a person like that.

"I just want some resolution." She didn't finish her sandwich and instead crumbled the rest of it in the parchment paper wrapping. "It's driving me crazy not knowing what's going on."

"I understand that." He reached across the table and squeezed her hand.

Jimmy James still couldn't believe that Kenzie returned his feelings. He planned on relishing every moment of her affection.

In fact, he felt a dopey smile on his face every time he thought about their kiss. She was entirely out of his league . . . but he wasn't complaining.

As Jimmy James heard footsteps crunching across the gravel, he glanced behind him and spotted a man he'd never seen before walking toward them. He had dark hair that was graying at the edges, a slim build, and olive skin.

He almost resembled . . .

"Mackenzie?" The man paused at their table.

Kenzie quickly withdrew her hand from Jimmy James' as she gasped. "Dad?"

A knot formed in Jimmy James' throat.

What was her dad doing here?

Suddenly, all his warm feelings vanished.

"WHAT ARE YOU DOING HERE?" Kenzie jumped to her feet, still in disbelief that her dad was in Lantern Beach.

She knew she shouldn't feel appalled at his appearance. Yet that was the best word to describe how she felt.

She hadn't seen her dad in more than a month, and every conversation since then had been tense.

Her father put his hands on his hips. "I came to find you."

"To find me? You knew where I was. Here in Lantern Beach. Why take the long trip?"

His intense gaze burned into hers. "I came here so I could take you home with me."

Outrage flushed through Kenzie. Her father had a lot of nerve. A *lot* of nerve.

She pressed her feet into the ground. "I'm not going home. We've been through this."

"I'm not going to let you throw your life away like this. You have a bright future. That doesn't include you hopping on boats and waiting hand and foot on other people." The words came out with a touch of bitterness and a whole lot of disdain.

"I told you I don't want to be a doctor." She crossed her arms and shook her head. "You're not going to change my mind."

Her father's gaze traveled across the picnic table to Jimmy James and his eyes narrowed. "Who is this?"

Jimmy James stood and offered his hand. "I'm Jimmy James."

Kenzie's father only stared at his outstretched hand before turning up his nose.

Finally, Jimmy James lowered his arm back to his side.

But as her father's gaze went back to Kenzie, she saw realization wash over him.

His fatherly instincts seemed to pick up on the fact that she and Jimmy James were more than friends.

"You're going to throw away everything for this guy?" The words came out like a bark as her father threw his hands in the air in an unusual display of emotion. "Is that what this is about?"

The sharpness of his words caused Kenzie to suck in a quick breath. Her heart hammered into her chest. "Dad . . . don't do this."

He looked back at Jimmy James again before scoffing. "What are you? A fisherman? A dockhand?"

"Don't answer that, Jimmy James," Kenzie rushed. "It's none of his business."

"Jimmy James, huh?" Derision dripped from his voice as he repeated the name. Her father turned back toward her and shook his head. "What are you going to do, Mackenzie? Live in a little shack with this guy? Have a future where you're always worrying about where you're going to get money for food and where your next paycheck is going to come from?"

"Dad, that's not fair—"

Her father shook his head again, not bothering to hide his vast disappointment in her choices. "Why would you want that for your future? You're too smart for that."

She felt the fire in her gaze grow stronger. "You don't know what you're talking about. My future is mine to decide. Not yours."

Jimmy James pointed behind him. "I should get back to the office. Unless . . . you want me to stay."

Kenzie shook her head. It was better if Jimmy James wasn't here for this conversation anyway. Who knew what kind of insults her father might continue to throw out?

"I'll talk to you later," she rushed.

"Thank you for lunch." He picked up their trash and nodded, an unreadable expression on his face.

As he walked away, she and her father stared at each other, and she knew a battle of wills was coming.

CHAPTER EIGHT

AS JIMMY JAMES strode toward the marina office, he tried not to let Kenzie's father's words bother him. But how could he not?

Especially since they were true.

He didn't want to admit it. He didn't want to think that the man's predictions might be correct. But he'd be a fool if he denied the truth in Dr. Anderson's statements.

Kenzie *could* have a great life with a successful, stable career while living in a nice house. Where she could raise children who would go to top schools and get all the best things in life.

If she stayed here with him in Lantern Beach and remained on course with the plans she'd made, her life would be much different. There would be few luxuries. Probably a lot of struggles. But she'd have a community that surrounded her and supported her through it all.

Besides, what about what Tom had said earlier? Bad company corrupts good character. Jimmy James would never want to corrupt Kenzie. But was that exactly what he might do?

He tried to put the thought out of his head. He really needed to get back to work. Plus, he sensed that Kenzie could use some privacy with her father.

Their talk should be between the two of them, and Jimmy James had nothing to do with it. Nor had he and Kenzie been together for long enough for Jimmy James to have any kind of say-so.

But those platitudes didn't stop the heaviness from pressing on his heart.

He opened the door to the marina office and paused when he heard voices drifting from the harbormaster's office.

"I don't want anyone to find out about this," Stevie-o muttered.

"My lips are sealed."

Jimmy James glanced over in time to see Thatcher hand Stevie-o an envelope. Stevie-o opened it, revealing a wad of green bills.

Thatcher was paying Stevie-o to do something secret for him.

Jimmy James felt his muscles tighten. He quietly stepped back outside and shut the door. He composed himself before stepping back in, trying to make it look as if he'd just walked up.

Thatcher paused in front of him before giving him a dirty look. "I was hoping I wouldn't see you again."

Jimmy James felt his muscles tighten. "Ditto."

"If you'll excuse me." Thatcher stormed toward him.

As he did, Jimmy James threw out his shoulder. Thatcher collided with it and scowled before continuing past.

When he was gone, Jimmy James turned to Stevie-o. "Everything okay?"

Stevie-o rubbed his beard and nodded. "Of course."

But his actions and words didn't match up.

What exactly was going on here? Someone was hiding something.

And Jimmy James was feeling more and more determined to figure out who and what.

———

"I'M NOT TALKING about this anymore." Kenzie stared at her dad from across the picnic table. "I'm sorry you came all this way, but I'm not changing my mind. I can't believe you thought I would."

Her father frowned, disappointment practically

dripping from his gaze. "I had to give it a shot. I'm really worried about you. Is it because of Leesa?"

Kenzie felt her lungs tighten at the mere mention of her stepmom's name. "You have to know that she doesn't like me."

"That's not true. She likes you." But even her father didn't sound convinced as he said the words.

"She wants you all to herself, Dad. And frankly, I'm tired of fighting this battle. You shouldn't have to choose between the two of us."

"But Mackenzie . . . you're my daughter . . ." He reached for her but dropped his arm instead.

"You picked Leesa to be your wife. I'm out of the house now, but you have to live with her." The words sounded harsh, but they were true. Kenzie had forced herself to come to terms with them not long ago. She'd had more peace in her life since then.

Her father opened his mouth and then shut it again. There was nothing he could say. Kenzie's words were true, and he couldn't deny them.

"Please, think about this." His voice cracked. "Don't give up everything—especially not for that guy."

She drew in a sharp breath at his words. "That guy?"

"You know what I mean." He rolled his eyes to the side.

"I just met *that guy*. I didn't come here to be with

him. I didn't take this career to be with him. Jimmy James is just a bonus."

Her father raised his eyebrows. "A bonus? If anything, I'd think someone like him would be a detriment."

"Someone like him?" Kenzie practically screeched. "Do you have any idea how entitled you sound?"

"I'm just speaking the truth." He shrugged unapologetically.

Defensiveness rose inside her until she felt like she couldn't breathe. "You don't know him. He's a good man."

"All I have to do is look at him, and I know enough."

Kenzie shook her head, unable to believe that her father would act like this. Yet he was.

She stepped back, making no effort to hide her disgust. "I have to get to work. Our charter should be leaving tomorrow."

"Mackenzie . . . please, think about what I said. You'll come to your senses one day and realize I'm right."

She raised her chin, unable to bring herself to agree. Instead, she brushed his words off and asked, "Are you staying here in Lantern Beach tonight?"

His cheek twitched as if he fought a frown. "I'm heading back to Delaware tomorrow. I'm staying in

Nags Head for the evening. I have to be back for surgery tomorrow afternoon."

"Of *course*." She hadn't meant for her words to sound bitter. The work her father did was important.

And it had always come before his family.

"Well, I'm sorry you came all this way for nothing." And before her dad could say anything else to her, Kenzie hurried toward *Almost Paradise*.

With any luck, Eddie and the rest of the crew would get here early.

But, mostly, she just wanted to get away from her dad.

CHAPTER NINE

JIMMY JAMES GRABBED some extra fishing line for Tom from his truck before heading back toward the docks. As he did, he nearly collided with Kenzie's dad.

His shoulders rolled back as he anticipated whatever might happen next.

"You need to stay away from my daughter." Dr. Anderson's voice sounded at a low growl.

"Respectfully, that's not your choice."

"If you care about her—and I think you do—you'll want what's best for her. And what's best for her is to come back to Delaware and finish her medical degree. It's not too late for her to continue with her classes in the fall. This . . ." He glanced around as if he couldn't find the words for the harbor. "This kind of life isn't what she was meant to do."

The man hadn't directly insulted Jimmy James, but his tone made it clear that's exactly what he'd done. "Kenzie feels differently about that."

"She's just going through a rebellious phase, and when it's over, she'll see that I'm right. Then she'll leave you behind . . . as she should."

Jimmy James stiffened. He didn't like this man.

Jimmy James knew Dr. Anderson was just being protective of his daughter. But he'd crossed some lines with this conversation.

"Think about what I said. You'll thank me later— when you discover I saved you a lot of heartbreak." The doctor pulled out his keys and hurried to his black Land Rover.

"I doubt that," Jimmy James muttered.

Kenzie's father hopped into his SUV and drove away.

But, in the man's short visit here, he'd left enough chaos and destruction to last for months . . . for Jimmy James at least.

EDDIE and the rest of the crew weren't as early as Kenzie had hoped they might be.

Instead, she stood just out of sight from her

father near *Almost Paradise* until she spotted him walking toward his vehicle. Then she checked inside the office for Jimmy James, feeling desperate to talk to him. But he wasn't there.

Kenzie finally spotted him walking back from the parking lot.

Relief swept through her.

Good. All she wanted to do was to talk to him, to apologize for the conversation he'd had to listen to. For what her father had said.

But when she saw her father's car pulling away, her relief turned into a surge of alarm.

Had Jimmy James and her father spoken again?

Her heart thudded at the thought before immediately quickening with panic.

She prayed that wasn't the case.

Because there was no telling what her father might have said . . . although she had a good idea. Or a *bad* idea, she should say.

She hurried toward Jimmy James and met him on the docks.

"I'm so sorry that you had to hear all of that," she rushed.

But Jimmy James kept walking, a new aloofness about him. Kenzie had to fall into step beside him to keep up as he headed toward his friend's boat.

"Maybe your father did the right thing by

coming here," Jimmy James muttered, still staring straight ahead.

She gulped in a quick breath, realizing what had happened.

Her father had gotten to him, just as she feared.

Kenzie grabbed Jimmy James' arm and pulled him to a stop. "You know that's not true."

He paused and stared at her, unreadable emotions in his eyes. What was that? Self-deprecation? Hurt? Longing?

"But do I?" he finally said.

No! That wasn't what she wanted to hear. She hadn't thought Jimmy James was the type to succumb to her father's pushiness. But her father had mastered the art of getting exactly what he wanted.

"Jimmy James . . . don't let him mess with your head. My father is a good man. But he feels his way is the right way—the *only* way. Maybe that's what you want in a world-renowned surgeon, someone who has that cockiness. It's great in the operating room but not so great in relationships."

Jimmy James seemed to break out of his tumultuous trance. He shook his head, almost as if sobering up. "I don't know what to think anymore."

Kenzie squeezed his arm again, feeling like something precious was slipping away from her. She hated the helpless feeling that came with it. "Jimmy James, please. Don't listen to him."

She stared up at him, their gazes locking. She hoped she'd gotten through to him. But she couldn't be sure.

He licked his lips and opened his mouth to say something. But as he did, his phone rang. He frowned as he looked at the screen.

He held the device up to show her. "It's Mr. Robertson."

Kenzie's breath caught. Mr. Robertson owned *Almost Paradise*. Why would he be calling Jimmy James?

Kenzie held her breath as he answered.

But she wasn't done with this conversation. She was nowhere close.

CHAPTER TEN

A FEW MINUTES LATER, Jimmy James shoved his phone back in his pocket and turned to Kenzie. The timing on that phone call couldn't have been better . . . or worse.

He wasn't sure which one it was yet. Too many thoughts were colliding in his head right now. His heart wanted one thing, and his mind wanted another.

And seeing Kenzie in front of him now . . . she made him want to give up everything and anything to make her happy. To put a smile on her face.

But he had to think about things in the long-term.

Which was why Mr. Robertson's call may have been an answer to prayer.

His throat burned as he said, "It looks like I have the answer that we are looking for."

Kenzie twisted her head, confusion floating in her gaze. "What does that mean?"

"Mr. Robertson asked me if I would captain the upcoming charter. He lost confidence in the other captain he had lined up, and he said he wants to give me another chance instead."

"That's . . . great." But Kenzie's voice lacked enthusiasm.

"If I'm the captain on the boat and you're one of the stewards, then we can't be together anyway. Any type of relationship would be inappropriate."

"Jimmy James . . ." She sent him a pleading look.

Grief clutched his heart until he felt an ache there. But he pushed it aside. "You know it's true. We can't have a romantic relationship on the boat if we're going to be working together."

She opened her mouth as if she wanted to say something then shut it again. Emotions raced through her gaze.

When she spoke again, her voice sounded hard. "You're right. I guess that's our answer."

Jimmy James' heart pounded in his ears. That response wasn't what he wanted. Not at all.

But Kenzie's father's voice wouldn't get out of his head. *If you really care about her then you know that this is what is best.*

And Jimmy James *did* really care about Kenzie. That's what made all of this even harder.

KENZIE COULDN'T BELIEVE she and Jimmy James were having this conversation.

It seemed surreal how quickly things had gone from happy and blissful to being turned completely upside down.

But if Jimmy James wasn't willing to fight for her then she didn't want to be with him anyway. Maybe it was better if the two of them discovered this now.

Yet, despite her resolve, grief still clutched her heart.

She'd really liked Jimmy James. She'd honestly thought there could be something special between them.

But he was right. If he was the captain and she was a steward, then it appeared they had their answer.

The beautiful romance that had started to blossom between them had ended as quickly as it had begun.

Jimmy James nodded at *Almost Paradise* before offering an apologetic shrug. "I'm sorry, Kenzie. But if I'm going to captain this boat, then I have a lot of stuff I need to get lined up."

She held back a sigh, feeling her heart harden in an effort to protect herself. "Of course."

Jimmy James took a step away but paused and turned to her. "Maybe we should both take some time to think things through."

She nodded as she felt herself shutting down—a protective measure she'd learned to master ever since her mother had died and her father remarried. When she'd moved to Lantern Beach, she had vowed to put that trait behind her. Apparently, that was easier said than done.

"You're right." Her voice sounded scratchier than she would have liked. "Maybe that is a good idea."

Jimmy James offered her another lingering glance. "I should go."

"The meeting is in about half an hour. I'll see you there."

As Jimmy James headed toward *Almost Paradise*, Kenzie sighed and walked toward her car. But, instead of climbing inside, she leaned against the door.

She needed to stop thinking about Jimmy James. It would do no good to mourn what had happened between them. Nor would it do any good to let bitterness well up inside her concerning her father.

She needed to focus her thoughts on something else.

Like last night's crime. It seemed like the perfect distraction.

She glanced around the marina, wondering what kind of secrets this place was hiding.

Her gaze went to *Seas the Day* again. What happened on that boat last night? She wasn't losing her mind. A woman was dead, and justice might not ever happen for her.

As the thoughts flittered through her head, Kenzie froze.

Someone was on that boat right now.

But she'd seen Thatcher leave. So, who was onboard?

Ducking behind various cars, Kenzie crept closer. She didn't want the person onboard to see her —or anyone else, for that matter. Thankfully, this wasn't a busy time at the marina.

She paused behind a truck and saw a man walking on the upper deck, a cloth in his hands. He paused right where Kenzie had seen the incident happen last night.

He began polishing the railings.

Anger ripped through her.

Was he trying to conceal any evidence before the police came back onboard?

Kenzie didn't know for sure. But it seemed like a real possibility.

The answer as to what had happened last night

had to be on that boat. Kenzie knew Cassidy and her officers had checked it over. But what if they'd missed something because they didn't know exactly what they were looking for?

A few minutes later, the man disappeared inside the cabin.

Kenzie continued watching until she saw the same man leave the boat five minutes later and head toward his car. She didn't recognize him with his dark baseball cap pulled down low over his face.

Who could he be? A member of the crew?

That was Kenzie's best guess.

As he drove away a few minutes later, a new thought hit Kenzie.

No one was around watching her right now. What if she quickly slipped onto *Seas the Day* and checked things out for herself? Maybe she'd see something no one else did—something that proved that woman had been murdered.

Even as the question fluttered through her head, Kenzie knew it was a bad idea. But that didn't stop the driving compulsion for her to follow through. To check out that boat and see if there was evidence hidden there.

She glanced around once more and still didn't see anyone.

If she was going to do this, here was her chance.

She couldn't think about her options too long or she'd miss the opportunity.

What should I do?

She knew the answer.

She should be brave. Shouldn't let others dictate her life. Shouldn't let rules act as roadblocks for justice.

Drawing a deep breath, she darted toward the boat.

This probably wasn't her smartest move.

But she prayed she didn't regret it.

CHAPTER ELEVEN

JIMMY JAMES LEANED back in his chair behind the helm of *Almost Paradise*.

He should feel happy considering he was getting to captain this superyacht again. In a way, he was. At least he'd get to be around Kenzie.

Except Kenzie probably wouldn't want to be around him anymore, and he couldn't blame her for that.

His mixed feelings made his insides feel like they were being ripped apart.

In the end, he kept coming back to Kenzie's father's words.

If you really care about her then you know that this is what is best.

He let out a sigh and tried to focus on the preference sheet Mr. Robertson had sent him.

Eight guests would be coming aboard for a three-day, two-night cruise. The primary guest was a guy named Kurt Stephens. He'd developed a game app called Fruit Cocktail Mafia and had just hit one million in sales. To celebrate he was bringing family and a few friends onboard.

Apparently, Kurt was a personal friend of Mr. Robertson. That only added more pressure to Jimmy James as the captain. He was confident if Kurt didn't find things up to par that he'd report it to Mr. Robertson—which wasn't fair, considering that Jimmy James was stepping in at the last minute.

But he didn't have time to think about that. Right now, he simply needed to get everything lined up for this trip. He only had thirty minutes until the rest of the crew arrived. This evening they'd need to get the boat ready for their guests, who were coming the next day.

When he finished reviewing everything and making some notes, he headed back outside. He wanted to be waiting on the docks when everybody arrived.

As he stood there, Stevie-o headed his way. Jimmy James remembered the conversation he'd overheard earlier and felt himself bristling.

Could Stevie-o have something to do with what Kenzie had seen happen? Could he be accepting money to cover it up?

"I'm glad I ran into you." Stevie-o paused in front of him and lowered his voice.

"Is that right?"

Stevie-o pulled his sunglasses down and turned a piercing gaze on Jimmy James. "If I were you, I'd stay away from Thatcher Davenport."

Jimmy James raised his chin, not fond of the threatening sound of Stevie-o's tone. "Why is that?"

"I know you're asking around about his boat. But he's not someone who should be messed with."

"You haven't gotten yourself tangled up in something you shouldn't, have you?" Jimmy James waited for his answer, not breaking his gaze.

Stevie-o's eyes narrowed. "I don't know what you're talking about. And whatever you think you know, forget about it."

Without saying anything else, Stevie-o stormed away.

What was that about? What was going on between Stevie-o and Thatcher?

Whatever it was, it could hold some of the answers he and Kenzie were looking for.

KENZIE FELT a rumble of nerves vibrate through her muscles as she darted onto *Seas the Day* and through the sliding glass door.

She shouldn't be on this boat. She knew she shouldn't. If she was caught . . . she could go to jail.

Or even worse.

What if the killer from last night returned and finished Kenzie off also? If this guy was as skilled as he appeared to be, he'd be able to hide the crime and her body would never be found.

Despite that, she remained on the boat, her heart hammering into her chest.

Seas the Day was half the size of *Almost Paradise*. The accommodations were nice, but she'd seen better, which surprised her. Thatcher seemed like the type who liked the best of the best.

The boat had three levels. The lower level held the engine room and some storage space. The middle level held the bridge, living area, and staterooms. The top deck was more of a party and entertaining area.

Kenzie really wanted to go to the top deck to look for evidence. But anyone could see her there—she'd be exposed—and she couldn't risk that.

Instead, she wandered through the main salon, looking behind the couches, in the drawers, and under tables.

She found nothing. Everything appeared so clean that it nearly felt uninhabited.

Next, she headed into the master stateroom. She

wondered if this was where Thatcher stayed. It made the most sense.

Various items had been scattered on the dresser there, leading her to believe he'd been staying here while he was in town. At least, he'd been staying when he wasn't visiting his friends at their rental house.

As before, she went through the various drawers then looked under the bed.

But she found nothing.

So far, this uninvited visit to the boat appeared to be wasted.

Kenzie paused in the center of the room and glanced around.

There had to be something here. What was she missing?

She paused at a photo on the dresser. She didn't allow herself to pick it up. Instead, she leaned closer to it.

It was a photo of Thatcher with a woman. Most likely his wife.

But the woman looked about thirty pounds over-weight and petite. That didn't match the description of the woman Kenzie had seen last night.

She stored that information away in the back of her mind. Was it significant? She wasn't sure. But she wanted to think about it more.

A noise in the distance caught her ear. Was that . . . a door sliding open?

Her heart raced.

Someone was here.

Was it Thatcher?

Or the killer?

Or maybe Thatcher *was* the killer . . .

Kenzie quickly glanced around, her heart racing out of control.

What should she do?

Whatever it was, she needed to decide quickly.

CHAPTER TWELVE

JIMMY JAMES GLANCED at the circle of people around him. All the crew members were here . . . everyone but Kenzie.

Had she gotten upset and left?

He didn't think Kenzie was the type to do that. Then again, the two of them didn't know each other that well. Still, Jimmy James had trouble thinking about where she could be if not here.

He observed the group surrounding him.

Eddie Ramos would pull double duty, serving as the first mate who helped operate the boat when Jimmy James wasn't on the bridge as well as the bosun.

Owen Hemlock was also a deckhand who'd keep the outside of the boat clean as well as handle any water toys their guests wanted to use while in route.

Sunni Briggs served as the chief steward. She oversaw the interior—including hospitality and all housekeeping as well as helping serve meals.

Kenzie would be the second stew, whenever she arrived here.

And Chef Durango was their cook. He had a French accent, but Kenzie had confided in Jimmy James that it was fake. Apparently, Kenzie had called him out on that during their last charter. He told her he used it so people would take his culinary skills more seriously.

The only new person in the group was a man named Pat Reynolds who'd serve as their new engineer as well as helping with other tasks on the boat.

Jimmy James glanced at his watch and saw that Kenzie was ten minutes late. He let out a breath, remembering that he couldn't show her any favoritism just because he was starting to fall in love with her.

Starting to fall in love with her?

That thought was ridiculous—and not true. It was too soon to fall in love. Besides, just as quickly as they'd gotten together, they'd broken up.

Things were over.

He glanced at his watch one more time before clearing his throat and turning to the crew. They all stood on the dock in front of *Almost Paradise*, and the heat felt sweltering without any shade.

No one would want to stand here very long, and he couldn't blame them.

"Let's go ahead and get started," Jimmy James said. "We don't want to run out of time."

"Where's Kenzie?" Eddie glanced around, his gaze concealed by his sunglasses, but his voice sounding genuinely confused.

"She should be here any minute," Jimmy James said.

Eddie's eyebrows flickered up as if that news surprised him.

Jimmy James sucked in a deep breath before running through some information on their guests, their itinerary, and the requested menu. When he finished, he disbursed everybody to begin their assigned tasks.

Then he glanced around the marina one more time.

His gaze stopped on Kenzie's car, which was still parked in the lot, right where she'd left it this morning.

Jimmy James' spine stiffened.

If her car was here and she wasn't, then something was wrong.

He had to find Kenzie.

His gut told him that she was in trouble.

KENZIE RACED from the master stateroom, into the hallway, and froze.

Where should she go now?

She couldn't risk darting to the main salon. She'd be caught if she did.

Glancing behind her, she saw only one viable option.

She rushed to the stairway leading below into the area where the engine room and storage closets were located.

Reaching the bottom, Kenzie frantically glanced around. She needed a place to hide, and she needed to find it quickly.

A door in the distance caught her eye. That was going to have to work.

She rushed toward it, threw it open, and a small closet stared back at her.

Knowing she didn't have much time, she slipped inside and pulled the door closed. She then pressed herself against the wall and held her breath, making a conscious effort not to move any more than necessary. The last thing she wanted was to give away her presence here.

Doing so would be a death wish.

Her heart pounded in her ears.

Kenzie should have never come aboard this boat. She'd known better. What had she been thinking?

Just stay still. Just stay still.

She continued to listen as footsteps pounded above her. She tried to imagine who it might be.

Thatcher? Or someone else?

She tried to picture what this person might be doing. Did he—the footsteps were heavy, leading her to believe it had to be a male—have any idea that Kenzie was onboard?

She didn't know.

As silence fell, she remembered the phone in her pocket. She could call for help!

But from whom?

Jimmy James had just broken up with her before they were even official.

She could call Cassidy, but then she'd have to admit she sneaked onto a boat.

She nibbled her lip and decided to wait.

Instead, she turned on the flashlight app and shone the beam around the space.

Mostly cleaning supplies surrounded her. In the corner, a rack stood with a broom and a mop. A shelf in front of her contained various sponges and rags. A small box had been shoved onto the bottom shelf.

Though Kenzie willed herself not to move, the sight of something lacy protruding from the box drew her curiosity.

Why would there be something lacy in a cleaning closet?

Against her better instincts, Kenzie leaned

forward and tugged the box from the shelf. Grabbing the edge of the item with just the tips of her fingers, she lifted it from its container.

It was lingerie . . . lacy black lingerie.

There was nothing wrong with lingerie, she supposed.

But hiding lingerie in a cleaning closet aroused her suspicions. Somebody was clearly trying to hide this negligee.

But why? The only reason Kenzie could think of was . . . if somebody was having an affair and didn't want his wife to see this.

Kenzie's heart pounded harder.

Was that what had happened? Had that woman on the deck last night been a secret lover? And had Thatcher tried to get rid of the woman in order to cover up their involvement together?

Kenzie didn't know, but that theory made the most sense right now.

As she heard a footstep overhead, she dropped the lingerie back into the box on the shelf and pressed herself against the wall again.

She went to turn off her flashlight when the phone slipped out of her hands.

She gasped as it tumbled behind the shelf. The flashlight flickered off before she could find the device.

But that was the least of her problems right now.

Had the person above her heard the phone drop? She froze.

She heard the footsteps again, but this time they were closer.

Really close.

Whoever was on the boat had come downstairs, she realized.

She had a feeling he was right outside her door.

Kenzie's throat tightened.

If this man found her, what would he do with her?

Every possibility that fluttered through her mind caused her anxiety to ratchet up. Her theories ranged from being sent to jail . . . to being killed.

She didn't like either of those extremes.

CHAPTER THIRTEEN

JIMMY JAMES STRODE around the harbor, asking everyone he ran into if they'd seen Kenzie. There weren't that many people here, but those he did encounter each said no.

He paused on the docks and placed his hands on his hips as he glanced around the area, trying to figure out his next step. As he did, the sun beat down on him and seagulls squawked overhead, circling as if they thought he had their next meal.

He frowned.

He knew Kenzie was mad at him—and rightfully so. But would she have done something foolish as a result?

He didn't think so, didn't think it was in her character. But . . . he felt more and more unsettled by the moment.

Should he call Kenzie?

Maybe. But he would hold off for now. She probably wouldn't welcome a call from him—she might not even answer.

Should he call Chief Chambers?

Jimmy James shook his head. Not yet.

He didn't want to overreact here.

He'd only been on the bridge for thirty minutes before his meeting with the crew. That wasn't much time—but probably enough for trouble to strike.

Kenzie had been in the parking lot before he boarded *Almost Paradise*. Where could she have gone?

What if her father had picked her up? Maybe the two of them had gone to grab coffee together or maybe she'd gone back with him.

It was a possibility.

But why would she leave her car?

She wouldn't.

Jimmy James wasn't accustomed to thinking in worst-case scenarios, but right now, he couldn't seem to stop himself.

That settled it. He was going to call her.

He *was* her captain so it wouldn't be out of line for him to see where she'd gone instead of coming to the meeting.

Before Jimmy James dialed her number, he

glanced around one more time. His gaze stopped on *Seas the Day*.

His stomach turned as he stared at the boat. Why did all the trouble in this area seem to go back to that boat right now? And what exactly had happened onboard last night?

Part of him wanted to brush it off and pretend Kenzie hadn't seen anything. But he didn't think that was the case, especially since someone had tried to run them down.

Still, he had a lot of questions.

If a woman had been killed, what happened to her body? How had the crime been covered up so quickly?

He remembered seeing a boat in the water last night, the one without any lights on. Was that a coincidence?

He was inclined to think that it wasn't.

Wasting no more time, he grabbed his phone, dialed Kenzie's number, and waited.

SWEAT TRICKLED down Kenzie's temples as she pressed herself against the wall.

Unfortunately, there wasn't a lock inside this closet. So, someone could easily open the door . . . and she'd be cornered.

Her pulse quickened. She should have never done this. Then again, she'd known that before she ever boarded this boat. That's why her father had always told her not to make impulsive choices. Even with his overbearing tendencies, he could be right sometimes.

She pressed her eyes shut, hardly able to breathe.

Then she heard footsteps again . . .

The paces paused outside the closet door.

Kenzie was certain of it.

She squeezed her eyes together even harder as she envisioned a man on the other side wearing all black and staring at the door with malice.

Maybe . . . maybe this guy would walk away. Maybe he'd never discover Kenzie was hidden here. Eventually, maybe she could slip out and make it back to *Almost Paradise*.

Wait . . . *Almost Paradise*.

The breath left her lungs.

She was supposed to meet with the crew.

What time was it?

She wasn't sure, but she felt certain the meeting had already started.

When Jimmy James noticed Kenzie wasn't there, what would he do? Would he look for her? Or was he still too upset over the conversation with her dad to take any action?

She nibbled on her lip for a minute, unsure of the answer.

Come on . . . move!

It sounded like the footsteps outside the door had been paused forever. What was this guy doing? Did she really want to know?

As the thought entered her mind, she heard the footsteps start again. The paces . . . they almost made it sound like the person on the other side was moving away from the closet.

Kenzie released a breath. Maybe she wouldn't go to jail or die after all.

Just then, her cell phone chirped on the floor.

Panic rushed through her.

Quickly, she reached for it, the lit screen guiding the way and desperation fueling her actions.

How could she have been so stupid? She should have put it on silent.

She reached behind the shelf until her fingers reached the device.

She quickly hit the button and the phone went quiet.

The question was, was it too late?

CHAPTER FOURTEEN

JIMMY JAMES SCOWLED as he put his phone away.

Kenzie hadn't answered. That wasn't like her. When he'd called her in the past, she'd picked up right away. But, again, maybe she was upset with him. Or maybe she was involved in a deep conversation.

But the uneasy feeling wouldn't leave him.

He let out a sigh and scanned the marina around him one more time.

As he glanced at *Almost Paradise,* he saw Eddie and Owen on the deck, scrubbing the floors there. On occasion, they glanced at him as if wondering what he was doing.

Jimmy James wouldn't alert anybody that Kenzie

was missing. Not yet, he decided. Not until he was sure that she wasn't okay.

Maybe for now the best thing he could do was just to get back onboard *Almost Paradise* and wait for Kenzie to show up.

As he started that way, Tom emerged from the marina office and waved.

"I'm about to head back out," Tom said. "Sure wish you could come with me."

"Me too," Jimmy James said. "But Danny will do a good job for you."

Danny was a teen they'd been training as a first mate on some of the fishing boats around here. The sixteen-year-old was anxious for the extra work in the summer, so it had worked out well.

"I'm glad I ran into you," Tom said as he approached. "You were asking about Thatcher this morning, right?"

Jimmy James nodded. "Right . . ."

"I remembered something after we talked. When I was at Watermen's last night, I saw him there."

"Okay . . ." Jimmy James wasn't sure what his friend was getting at.

"This may not mean anything, but he was with . . . Stevie-o. The two were talking like they were old friends or something. They seemed like a mismatched duo if I've ever seen one."

His breath caught. "Is that right?"

Tom nodded. "Just thought I'd let you know. Everything else okay?"

"I suppose. You haven't seen Kenzie by chance, have you?"

"Kenzie?" Tom pushed his sunglasses up higher. "When I went back to my boat earlier, I thought I saw her."

His breath caught. "When was that?"

Tom shrugged. "Thirty or forty minutes ago probably."

Jimmy James' heart pounded harder. "Did you see where she was heading?"

"I can't say for sure. But unless my eyes were deceiving me, I thought she was walking toward *Seas the Day*." Tom nodded toward the boat.

Jimmy James' breath caught. That was what he was afraid of.

What if Kenzie had gone aboard that boat? What if her disappearance was somehow connected to last night's crime?

"Was she by herself?" Jimmy James rushed.

Tom shrugged again. "Maybe. But I really wasn't paying much attention. Sorry."

Jimmy James took his phone out again.

Should he call Cassidy?

Or should he check out *Seas the Day* himself?

KENZIE COULDN'T BREATHE. Her lungs were too tight. Her heart pounded too hard. Fear paralyzed her.

If someone hadn't known she was in this closet, they did now.

What was the person on the other side of the door doing?

The footsteps had paused again.

Think, Kenzie. Think!

She might be an intruder on somebody else's boat, but there could be a killer onboard. She couldn't just stand here helpless and wait for someone to harm her.

Moving quickly, she grabbed a bottle of cleaner from the shelf and clutched it to her chest. If someone opened the door and tried to hurt her, she would spray detergent in their face.

Maybe the act would buy her a few minutes. Long enough to get away. To run up the steps and call for help.

Speaking of help, who had called her? She'd slipped the phone back into her pocket. She could grab it again and try to call or text someone.

But then she wouldn't be prepared to spray the cleaner in someone's face when they opened the door.

She decided to keep hold of the cleaner instead.

At once, she heard something slide. Heard the jangle of metal.

More fear trickled down her spine.

Then there was silence.

Kenzie remained frozen, unsure what the best thing was to do. She halfway expected someone to open the door and grab her. She waited for what felt like an hour, but it was probably only five or ten minutes.

Were those footsteps again? Were they getting softer? Moving away from her?

That's what it sounded like.

She prayed that was the case.

Finally, when she didn't hear anything else, she reached for the doorknob and twisted it. Maybe now was the time she should try to escape.

But as she pushed on the door, it didn't open—not even a little.

She shoved harder.

But the door still wouldn't budge.

That's when Kenzie realized somebody had locked her in here. Maybe shoved something against the door or jammed something into the lock. She didn't know.

Fear ran down her spine, causing her entire body to tremble.

If she didn't get out of here . . . then she didn't know what would happen to her next.

CHAPTER FIFTEEN

JIMMY JAMES WAS GOING to board *Seas the Day*. He had no other choice.

He wouldn't call Chief Chambers—not yet, at least.

As he took a step closer, a man emerged from the salon onboard.

Jimmy James ducked back behind a fuel station and watched as the man walked down the gang-plank, crossed the slip, and continued past. This guy wore a dark hat that he kept pulled down low over his face, making it hard to see any of his features.

The man wasn't Thatcher. So, who was he? A member of the crew? A member of the security team? The man Kenzie saw last night?

Jimmy James had no idea.

He waited until the guy disappeared before

glancing around quickly to make sure nobody was watching. Then he hurried up the gangplank and stepped onto the boat.

If he got caught doing this . . . he would go back to jail.

His stomach clenched so hard at the thought that a moment of nausea rose in him.

This time, he might not get off easy. Police might look at his past record and decide he needed to stay in prison longer. Even though he considered Chief Chambers a friend, she probably wouldn't be able to call in any favors for him.

He knew the risks. But if Kenzie was on this boat . . .

Jimmy James slipped into the salon and glanced around.

No one was in here.

He checked the rest of the rooms on the main deck.

They were empty.

He hadn't seen Kenzie on the top deck, so that only left one more place.

The lower deck.

He drew in a deep breath before rushing down the small stairway. At the end, he paused.

A quick scan showed the area was empty.

Maybe Kenzie wasn't on this boat after all.

But as Jimmy James glanced at the closet in the

distance, he saw a small wooden chair had been wedged between the door handle and the opposite wall.

Strange.

The only reason anyone would do that was . . .

To keep someone inside the closet.

He rushed across the room, grabbed the chair, and shoved it out of the way.

Then he threw the door open.

Instead of seeing Kenzie, spray hit his face.

A burning sensation filled his eyes as he let out a yell.

What was going on?

"JIMMY JAMES?" Kenzie gasped, horror washing through her.

She dropped the spray bottle and rushed toward him. She'd sprayed him in the eyes with glass cleaner.

No, no, no!

Panic raced inside her as she realized what she'd done.

Quickly, she grabbed a roll of paper towels from the shelf and jerked several sheets from the roll. She patted his eyes, which were still squeezed shut.

The good news was, she'd only sprayed once

before she'd realized who it was. And Jimmy James' eyes closed just as quickly and . . .

"Are you okay?" Kenzie reached for him, resting her hand on his bicep as she studied his face, desperate to know she hadn't done too much damage.

He took the paper towel from her and wiped his eyes again. His entire face was scrunched as if he were in pain.

"What are you doing?" His words came out rapid, worried, irritated—all wrapped in one unmistakable tone. "It's just me."

"I'm sorry, Jimmy James. I thought the guy who locked me in there came back to . . . do who knows what." Her voice caught.

He blinked a few more times and then shook his head. His shoulders softened as he drew in a breath. "We don't have time to talk. Let's get you out of here."

Kenzie nodded quickly, almost frantically.

She was free . . . but at what cost?

Jimmy James blinked again before grabbing her hand. Then, moving more quickly than she thought was possible, he pulled her up the stairs. He paused at the top, glanced around, and then continued moving.

He didn't stop until they were off the boat and a good two hundred feet away from *Seas the Day*. As they paused on the dock, Kenzie searched the area for anyone who might have seen them.

Everyone appeared to be minding their own business.

She prayed that was the case.

"What were you thinking?" Jimmy James turned toward her, his eyes stormy. "Did you go on that boat of your own free will?"

How was she going to explain this to him? "I just needed to see if there was any evidence—"

"That was not a smart move." His eyes narrowed.

She crossed her arms, some of her guilt from spraying him in the face disappearing at his harsh tone. "I realize it wasn't a smart move."

"You could have gotten yourself killed, you know."

"I am very aware of that." Her voice continued to harden.

He stared at her another moment before shaking his head. Then his tone softened as he said, "I'm glad you're okay."

Kenzie sucked in a deep breath, trying to get her emotions under control. "Thank you for coming to get me."

"Did you see anything? Find any evidence?"

"I found some lingerie hidden in the closet. There's only one reason I can think of why Thatcher would hide that."

"Maybe because it doesn't belong to his wife?"

She nodded, a surge of satisfaction rushing through her at the realization she and Jimmy James were on the same page.

"Exactly," she whispered. "Should we call the police?"

"No. If Thatcher finds out that you were trespassing on his boat, he *will* press charges."

"But—"

"And if it comes out that I was trespassing on his boat also, then the police are going to throw the book at me. I already have a rap sheet. I have to stay clean, Kenzie."

She sucked in a breath. She hadn't thought about that. Her actions could have had dire consequences for Jimmy James. If she were arrested, her father would most likely bail her out.

Who did Jimmy James have to do that for him?

She licked her lips before finally saying, "I'm sorry. I never meant for any of this to happen. I definitely didn't want to pull you into it. I never expected you'd come onboard looking for me."

Jimmy James glanced around before stepping closer. "I know things are rocky with the two of us right now. But let's keep what happened between us."

"And the person who did this," Kenzie added

quietly. "Because there's a third person at play here —the person who locked me in that closet."

Jimmy James glanced behind her, his jaw tightening as if a bad memory had hit. "I saw a man, I'm guessing he was a security guard, leave the boat earlier—right before I boarded. He must be the one who locked you in that closet. I didn't see anyone else onboard."

"If you hadn't found me . . ." Her voice cracked.

What if she'd been stuck on that boat all night? If she hadn't been able to reach her phone or if it hadn't worked after being dropped?

What had that man planned on doing with her when he returned? She could have been taken out to sea. Beaten. Left for dead.

And no one would ever know.

She shivered again as she realized how dumb it had been for her to go on that boat.

Jimmy James started to reach for her but dropped his arm instead. "The important thing is that I *did* find you. But now, we need to keep moving forward as if this didn't happen. At least until we have a plan."

Kenzie nodded quickly and tried to shift her thoughts away from the fear that wanted to consume her. If only it were that easy. If she could just push a button and make that happen.

She sighed. "I understand. That makes sense."

He nodded toward *Almost Paradise*. "Great. Because the rest of the crew is wondering where you are right now. We don't want them asking too many questions."

"I'll just tell them I got held up with something. That my father unexpectedly came into town and threw me off schedule."

"Sounds good."

Kenzie frowned. Somehow, she was in over her head . . . again.

This was becoming a new normal for her, it seemed.

CHAPTER SIXTEEN

EVERYTHING INSIDE JIMMY JAMES screamed that he should report what happened to Kenzie. But he knew if he did that Thatcher would press charges. He had no doubt about that. If he was in jail, he'd be no good to Kenzie.

As he and Kenzie headed down the docks toward *Almost Paradise*, he remembered the man he'd seen leaving the boat earlier. Jimmy James needed to find out who he was. He had to be the guy who'd locked Kenzie in that closet.

That made him an enemy of Jimmy James.

He fisted his hands at his side.

He wished he had the privilege of pouring all his time and energy into figuring out what was going on here. But that wasn't a possibility. Especially now that he was the captain of *Almost Paradise*.

He and the crew still had a lot of work to do to get ready before their guests arrived. It wouldn't be fair to anybody if he didn't put his full attention into this charter. Not doing so could result in putting people in a different kind of danger.

As Kenzie walked beside him toward the boat, he resisted the urge to reach out and touch her. Holding her hand had felt so natural, and old habits were hard to break—even if those old habits had come on quickly.

He couldn't give in. He was not only her boss, but there was a vast divide between them.

His chest tightened at the thought of it. He should have known better than to get his hopes up that a relationship between them would work. He should have known better than to let himself believe that the two of them could have a chance.

It was better if they ended this now. There would be less heartache in the long run.

But that didn't mean he didn't feel regret.

"I feel like I should tell Cassidy," Kenzie muttered, still staring straight ahead as if afraid someone might be watching. "I don't want to tell her what I did. I just want to tell her what I saw."

"I know you do. But you can't. Besides, Cassidy couldn't use what you found as evidence. She would need a search warrant for anything to be admissible."

"You're right. But something dirty is going on aboard *Seas the Day*."

"Remember, you promised you'd leave this to the police."

Kenzie frowned as she nibbled on her lip. "I know. I've never thought of myself as being a particularly nosy person. But there's something about what happened that just won't allow me to let it go."

Jimmy James didn't like the sound of that.

He appreciated the fact that Kenzie desired justice for whoever may have been injured or killed last night. But he didn't like the idea of her putting herself in danger.

And that's exactly what she was doing.

As they stepped onto *Almost Paradise*, Jimmy James turned to her. There was something he needed to say before anybody else was around. "Do your best to put on a smile. The less people who know about what happened, the better."

"You mean, about being locked in the closet?"

"No, I mean about everything. I don't want you to be a target, and the more people who know that you saw a murder, the more desperate someone might become to silence you. Especially if you think this guy saw your face."

Kenzie's skin went pale, and she nodded.

But before they had time to talk, the rest of the crew surrounded Kenzie and greetings went around.

Maybe it was better that way. Because Jimmy James needed to get his mind straight right now.

"YOU WANT to come play a game of Spoons?" Eddie called across the salon. "Besides, how many times can you wipe down that table. It's clean. I think even Sunni will agree!"

Kenzie glanced at the rest of the crew as they settled down to play a card game after a long afternoon of getting the boat ready. Being a crewmember on the boat was quite possibly one of the most demanding jobs she'd ever done.

Kenzie knew staying busy had been good for her —which was probably why she didn't want to stop now. The tasks gave her something to occupy her thoughts, something other than what had happened aboard *Seas the Day*.

Yet all she wanted to think about was the dead woman. The lingerie in the closet. The person who'd locked her on that boat.

And Jimmy James breaking up with her after the conversation with her father.

She sighed, trying to push away the heaviness she felt.

"Kenzie?"

She paused and glanced at Eddie. "Sorry. I'm a

little distracted. I think I'll pass for tonight, but thanks for the invite. I still have a few more loads of laundry to wash anyway."

"Can't you do them later?" Sunni asked. "We have all night."

Kenzie shrugged. "Sorry. I can't relax until my work is done."

Tonight, the crew would sleep onboard so they could be here bright and early when their guests arrived.

She glanced around, wondering where Jimmy James had disappeared to. She hadn't seen him in the last hour.

Maybe that was good.

Because part of her felt like it died just a little every time she saw him. She wanted to be mad at him. Part of her *was* upset.

Then she remembered how he'd rescued her from the closet.

How could she be mad after that?

She knew Jimmy James cared about her. That was obvious. He cared about her so much that he was willing to give her up, thinking it was for the best.

But that wasn't what she wanted.

She wanted to see where their relationship could go. But he'd put the brakes on things before they'd barely started.

She grabbed a bottle of water and paced away from the rest of the crew. They were so deep into their game that they hardly noticed. She walked to the top deck, thankful the night had cooled the sizzling summer temperatures some.

She leaned on the railing and drank in a deep breath.

The place she'd chosen to stand just happened to face *Seas the Day*.

Except it wasn't happenstance.

Whenever she'd had a chance today, she'd stolen glances at the boat, looking for some type of clue as to what was going on.

Right now, the lights were on. She assumed that meant that Thatcher was back onboard.

This island didn't seem like the type of fancy, elite harbor he'd be drawn to. Besides, why had he traveled here on such a big boat if he was just visiting friends?

Kenzie had the impression a small crew worked for him, so coming here hadn't been a task done out of the love of trying to navigate these waters by himself.

She didn't know, but the whole situation bothered her.

When she spotted two figures on the dock in the distance, she paused.

She sank behind the railing where no one would see her unless they were directly looking.

Was that . . . her breath caught.

It was. It was Jimmy James.

He'd left their boat and was talking to someone. They were too far away for Kenzie to make out what they said.

Who was that man he was talking to? She didn't think she had ever seen him before.

He was tall and thin with dark hair and a bit of a bad boy vibe. He stood beside a motorcycle.

Was he someone from Jimmy James' past? One of the bad influences he'd talked about before?

The unsettled feeling in her gut churned harder.

The two of them shook hands before Jimmy James stepped back. He glanced around as if to make sure nobody was watching.

Kenzie's lungs froze.

What was he doing? Whatever it was, his actions looked sketchy.

She frowned. Of all the people on this boat, Jimmy James was the one she thought she could trust.

But what if she was wrong? What if Jimmy James had more demons from his past than he'd let on?

Kenzie didn't want to believe that was true.

But, based on his shady actions, she'd be a fool not to ask herself those questions.

CHAPTER SEVENTEEN

JIMMY JAMES WAS thankful their first night on the boat was uneventful. Given everything that had already happened, one never knew quite what to expect.

He'd awoken early and grabbed a quick breakfast—bacon and eggs prepared by Chef Durango. After welcoming the guests onboard and getting them settled, he disappeared onto the bridge to clear his head.

Kurt and his group didn't appear to be wild partiers like some others were. He'd brought his wife, four children, his brother, and his brother's wife. Most of their conversations revolved around tech and computers.

The itinerary for their three-day trip would take them down the North Carolina coast to Wilmington then to South Carolina to Myrtle Beach before heading back to Lantern Beach. The trip would be short but hopefully easy.

Before Jimmy James did anything else, he grabbed his phone and called Chief Chambers. He had a couple of questions for her before they got underway, starting with asking about any updates on the woman Kenzie had seen pushed off the boat.

"There haven't been any reports of any missing women on Lantern Beach," Chief Chambers said.

He frowned. "That's too bad—or it's a good thing, depending on how you look at it."

"I know. We're still keeping our eye on things, but so far there's been nothing."

He stared across the ocean, thankful for the nearly placid water they had today. At least, it was one thing to be thankful for. "Thanks for the update."

"No problem. There's one other thing I thought I would mention. I don't usually share details of my investigations, but since you and Kenzie seem to have a personal stake in this . . . I thought I'd let you know that Thatcher Davenport's alibi checks out."

Jimmy James sucked in a breath. "It does?"

"It does. I talked with the people he had dinner with, and they all verified he was there the entire time."

He frowned. Thatcher Davenport was his

number one suspect. However, the man seemed to have enough money to pay someone else to do his dirty work.

Cassidy seemed to read his mind. "I also looked into his two bodyguards. They were at a local restaurant throwing back some drinks at the time when the potential murder happened."

His frown deepened. "Good to know."

"Speaking of Kenzie, how is she doing? She was pretty shaken up last time I saw her."

He let out a long breath at the chief's question. How *was* Kenzie doing?

Jimmy James tried to think of a quick answer. But he couldn't.

Kenzie was clearly upset with him and shaken about yesterday's incident.

Finally, he cleared his throat and said, "She's hanging in, just as expected."

"That's good. Keep an eye on her. If the alleged killer really did see her face, then she could be a target."

He gripped the phone tighter. "Those were my thoughts exactly."

"Watch your back too. Because if she's a target, then you might be one too by association."

He ended the call and frowned. Just when he hoped life might get simpler, everything felt way too complicated again.

Jimmy James didn't have time to dwell on that now. He had a crew that was depending on him to lead them.

His only hope was that the friend he'd met with last night might have some information for him soon.

———

ALMOST PARADISE MADE it to Wilmington by midmorning. When they arrived, they docked at the harbor so Kurt and his crew could do a tour of the film area.

Wilmington—called Filmington by some—was the filming location for several movies and TV shows including scenes from *Iron Man 3, A Walk to Remember*, and *Dawson's Creek*. Many people found the area fascinating.

It wasn't just the filming sites that made it unique. The town was picturesque with its waterfront location on the Cape Fear River and the inclusion of the battleship *USS North Carolina* docked on its banks.

Kenzie had been asked to accompany the group on their outing along with Jimmy James and Owen.

She'd enjoyed herself. The group had even been able to see part of a show being filmed—one called *Relentless* featuring actress Joey Darling.

As she toured the town, she kept her eyes wide open.

She had no reason to believe anyone had followed her here. In fact, the thought was ridiculous. But Kenzie couldn't afford to let her guard down, considering everything that had happened.

To end the tour, the group stopped at an ice cream shop.

As the guests ordered their treats, Kenzie felt her phone nearly burning a hole in her pocket.

Every chance Kenzie got, she searched the internet for missing women. She'd started with searching this area. Then she'd moved to the whole East Coast. Now she'd broadened her search to missing women across the US. It was hard to narrow down where exactly that woman may have come from.

But Kenzie hadn't made her up.

She glanced around and saw that everyone was occupied. Then she slipped outside and leaned against the brick wall of the building to resume her search.

As she stood there, goosebumps popped up across her skin.

She froze before raising her head then glancing around, trying to find the cause of the reaction.

Was someone watching her?

She didn't see anyone.

She scanned her surroundings once more, but still couldn't pinpoint anything.

Swallowing hard, she turned back to her phone and scanned various headlines of missing women before stopping on one.

The breath left her lungs.

This woman could be the one.

It was hard to say for sure since Kenzie hadn't been able to make out the woman's features. But, still, something about the woman—the way she looked and her slim build—raised all kinds of flags in Kenzie's mind.

Ashley Nelson. Twenty-five years old. From Indiana. A law student and top scholar who volunteered for a local homeless shelter and had received awards for her service.

Kenzie scrolled through all the pictures she could find, looking for some kind of clue.

There was nothing—only photos of a happy law school student with a small lightning tattoo on her collarbone.

She nibbled on her lip. She had no way to prove it. But her gut told her this was the woman.

So, what was she going to do with this information? Would it be like that lingerie she'd found last night—useless? And, if so, how could she change that?

CHAPTER EIGHTEEN

AS KURT CONTINUED to talk to Jimmy James about his Fruit Cocktail Mafia game, Jimmy James glanced out the window of the ice cream shop.

Where had Kenzie gone? He'd seen her step outside, and part of him had wanted to follow her.

He'd stopped himself, trying not to be overprotective.

Instead, Jimmy James scanned outside the window, trying to smile and nod at Kurt as he talked ad nauseum about his game. Unfortunately, playing on his phone had never been Jimmy James' thing. He'd rather be outside fishing.

Finally, he spotted Kenzie leaning against the building, her phone in her hand and a tight expression on her face as she stared at the screen.

Something was wrong.

"So, I'm thinking about adding some more exotic fruits—"

Jimmy James raised a finger. "I hate to interrupt you, but could you excuse me a minute? There's something I need to check out."

Kurt shrugged and took another bite of his mango ice cream. "Of course. Of course."

Jimmy James wove between the tables then out the door toward Kenzie.

He paused beside her as she stood on the sidewalk. "Everything okay?"

She looked up at him, her gaze startled yet ignited as if she had discovered something. "You're going to think I sound crazy."

"What is it?"

"I've been scanning the headlines for missing women. I keep broadening my search. And just now, I found her." She held up her phone and showed him a picture of a missing woman named Ashley Nelson.

He sucked in a quick breath. Of all the things he'd guessed Kenzie might say, this wasn't one of them. "Why do you think it's this woman?"

"I don't know . . ." Kenzie shook her head before rubbing her temples with her free hand. "She just . . . she fits that description."

"I thought you couldn't see her well the night of the murder, that you couldn't make out any details?"

He eyed Kenzie more carefully, trying to get inside her head and figure out what she was thinking.

"I couldn't see her clearly. I could only see her profile, her silhouette."

Jimmy James didn't say anything for a moment. But the evidence seemed flimsy, like she was reaching a little too hard.

A frown tugged at Kenzie's lips. "You do think I'm crazy, don't you?"

"I don't think you're crazy. But I do feel like you might be overreaching right now. Why would this woman from Indiana be in North Carolina? Why would she be with Thatcher Davenport?"

Kenzie shook her head. "I don't know. I have no idea for that matter. Should I tell Cassidy?"

Jimmy James thought about it a moment, not wanting to lead Kenzie astray. But this was a leap. There was absolutely no proof that her theory was correct. They needed more information before they told anyone about this possibility.

"Let's go back to the boat and do some more research first," he finally said. "When does your shift end tonight?"

"I'm working until ten."

"Let's meet after that and see if we can find out some more details. Okay? Because we don't want to cry wolf. If we are going to tell Chief Chambers that this might be the girl then we need to have more proof. We need to look at this woman's social media posts. See if there's anything that connects her to North Carolina or Thatcher Davenport."

Kenzie nodded. "You're right. That *would* be the smartest thing to do."

Relief washed through Jimmy James at her easy agreement. He'd been halfway expecting an argument, another lapse of judgment like the one she'd had when she'd sneaked aboard *Seas the Day*.

"Okay then," he finally said. "I'll see you on the bridge somewhere around ten?"

"It's a deal."

He nodded to the charter guests inside the ice cream shop. "Now, let's get this group back on the boat so they can start getting ready for dinner."

KENZIE COULD HARDLY WAIT for dinner to be over. Although the beef tenderloin and fingerling potatoes had smelled savory and delicious, her mind was elsewhere.

She thought she'd done a decent job covering her anxiety as she served guests their food and refilled their drinks. But she couldn't be sure. Every time Kenzie allowed her mind to drift, she thought of the picture she'd seen of that woman.

More than anything, Kenzie wanted to sit down

with her computer and see what else she might discover.

But there was no time for that now.

When dinner was finished, their guests disappeared onto the aft deck for some late-night cocktails. Kenzie quickly helped in the kitchen, then worked on some laundry, and emptied several trashcans.

Finally, her shift ended.

She took a quick shower, changed, and then headed toward the bridge.

Dread filled her when she thought about seeing Jimmy James. Dread and excitement.

How could she feel both of those things about the man? He'd listened to Kenzie's father instead of listening to what she wanted. How could he do that to her?

She didn't know, but she didn't appreciate it either. Despite those hard feelings, another part of her still cared about Jimmy James more than she would like. Being around him was difficult, to say the least. Every time she saw him, she was reminded that he thought their different backgrounds would ultimately keep them apart.

Part of her wanted to try and convince him otherwise. But she didn't want to have to convince someone to be with her. She knew firsthand that when a person wanted something badly enough, they'd fight to get it.

Jimmy James' eyes lit with attraction as soon as he saw her, but the emotion quickly faded as if he pulled himself back in place. They were no longer a couple, and they probably never would be. Both of them needed to keep that at the forefront of their minds.

He raised his head. "You're late."

"I smelled like a mix of seabass and sweat, I'm afraid. I had to get cleaned up."

He didn't react to her statement. He only nodded toward a bench seat against the wall. "Why don't you have a seat, and we can do that research we talked about earlier?"

That sounded perfect to her. She only wished his tone didn't sound so aloof.

As Kenzie sat, she angled herself so she wouldn't be too close to Jimmy James. Another part of her wanted to scoot closer until she could smell the sandalwood scent of his soap. But that would be a very bad idea.

"So, let's see what we can find out about this Ashley Nelson lady." He pulled out his laptop and began typing, his thick fingers almost seeming too big for the keyboard. "Everything people are saying about her in the interviews make it sound like Ashley is a pretty clean and wholesome girl."

Kenzie leaned closer, desperate to see what he

was reading. "A clean and wholesome girl isn't likely to have an affair with someone like Thatcher, is she?"

"You're right. It's not beyond the realm of possibility, but it *does* seem unlikely."

Kenzie leaned back, still trying to sort out her thoughts so she could offer some direction or insight. "If Thatcher is an attorney, and Ashley is in law school then maybe that's the connection."

"Good theory." Jimmy James typed in a few more things before shaking his head. "It looks like she was in school up near Chicago. So that still doesn't provide us any connections."

Kenzie leaned back. She didn't want to admit that Jimmy James was right, but he was. There was absolutely no proof that Ashley Nelson was the woman she'd seen murdered.

"What about news articles about her disappearance?" Kenzie asked. "When was the last time she was seen?"

"According to this article, she was last seen three days ago. She told her family she was going to visit a friend down in Arkansas, but she never showed up." Jimmy James turned toward her and frowned. "I'm sorry, Kenzie. But I just don't know if this is enough to tell Cassidy about her."

Again, she wanted to argue. But she couldn't because Jimmy James was right.

What Kenzie had was more of a whim than anything else.

How could she find proof?

She wasn't sure, but she wasn't ready to give up yet.

CHAPTER NINETEEN

AS SOON AS Kenzie left the bridge, Jimmy James grabbed his cell and called his friend. He kept an eye on the controls as he waited for an answer.

On the second ring, Axel Hendrix picked up. "Hey, man."

Axel was a former Navy SEAL who worked for Blackout, the private security organization Ty Chambers had cofounded.

Jimmy James had gotten to know Axel through their common interest in motorcycles. He'd asked Axel to meet at the docks last night. He had a job for his friend.

He didn't know what the going rate was for hiring Blackout—he hadn't asked—but he'd pay whatever necessary if it meant keeping Kenzie safe.

He'd asked Axel to do some background checks

on various people Jimmy James considered suspects. Axel was also keeping an eye on things at the harbor while Jimmy James wasn't there. Jimmy James was anxious for an update.

"Any headway?" Jimmy James felt his lungs tighten as he waited for what he might hear.

"I've been asking around, and I'm pretty sure one of these guys who works for Thatcher Davenport is Damon Hedges. He and his colleagues work as bodyguards and are based out of the Raleigh area. The other guy—Matt Davis—seems clean. But Damon..."

Axel's statement seemed to fit everything Jimmy James would have guessed about the two men he'd seen with Thatcher. "What about Damon? You know anything else about his background?"

"He spent five years in the military before being dishonorably discharged. From what I can tell, he has an assault charge on file. I suspect that's why he took this job."

Jimmy James frowned. "Has he been hanging out at the harbor anymore or did he leave?"

"I've been keeping my eye on the docks all day, and both Damon and Matt are still there. I've seen them and Thatcher together. I tried to strike up a conversation, but none of them seemed too talkative."

"Thanks. Your information helps give me a better

feel for the guy. I appreciate your help. And if anything else pops up, let me know."

"It's no problem," Axel said. "And I'll keep this between you and me."

"I appreciate it."

Jimmy James stared out over the water and locked his jaw in place.

He definitely had a lot to think about.

AS KENZIE LAY IN BED, she tried to rest—especially since she actually had some time alone. Sunni was working a later shift tonight, and Kenzie wasn't complaining about having their bunkroom to herself for a little while.

But instead of relaxing, her mind continued to race through everything that had happened.

She was going to go crazy if she kept thinking about that murder. That's why she wanted to find answers—so she could put her mind at ease.

Instead, trying to find answers was only serving to cause more trouble.

What was she supposed to do? Against her better instincts, she stared at a picture of Ashley with a woman named Merilee Foreman, who was tagged as her BFF in several pictures. On a whim, Kenzie searched for the woman's contact information.

She was surprised at how easily she found it.

She nibbled on her lip a moment before spontaneously dialing the number. Merilee answered on the first ring.

Kenzie sat up, wishing she had thought this through some more. "Merilee, my name is Kenzie. I know it's late to call, and I apologize. But I had a couple of questions about your friend Ashley."

"Have you seen her?" Excitement—and hope—lit the woman's voice.

"No, I haven't. Not really."

"Not really? What does that mean?"

Kenzie shook her head, realizing this conversation wasn't going well—and it had just begun. "I mean, I wondered if I'd seen her, but I'm not sure. Is there any chance she came to North Carolina?"

"North Carolina? Where in North Carolina?"

Kenzie swallowed hard, hoping she wasn't sharing too much. "Lantern Beach."

Merilee let out a soft grunt. "She never mentioned Lantern Beach. Why? Did you see her there?"

"I thought I might have, but I'm uncertain. I just . . . I just felt it impressed on me that I should ask, just in case." Kenzie paused, contemplating what to say next. "What about a man named Thatcher Davenport? Did Ashley ever mention him? Maybe she worked with him at his law practice or something?"

"The name doesn't ring any bells," Merilee said. "But I'll tell the police. Maybe they can check it out—"

"I don't have any proof of anything," Kenzie rushed, feeling panicky at the mention of the police. "I'm sure they get tons of false leads and—"

"Is there something you're not saying? Do you know more?"

Kenzie pressed her eyes closed. "No, I don't. I'm sorry. I shouldn't have called."

Before Merilee could ask any more questions, Kenzie hit End. She held the phone to her chest, her heart pounding out of control.

That had been a mistake. Not only did she not have any answers, now she'd potentially given Merilee false hope. She couldn't bring herself to tell Merilee that her friend may have been murdered.

Kenzie had just started to drift to sleep when her phone buzzed. She snatched it from her chest where it still rested and glanced at the screen.

Was it Merilee? Was she calling back to ask more questions?

Instead, Kenzie saw she'd gotten a text from an unknown number.

Out of curiosity, she clicked on the notice, figuring it was most likely junk.

But as the message filled her screen, a picture appeared.

Her gut clenched.

A picture of her. In Wilmington. Earlier today.

Somebody *had* been watching her.

This person had snapped a photo of Kenzie leaning against the wall at the ice cream shop and holding her phone. And this person was sending this to her so she could have no doubts that somebody was watching. This was a subtle threat.

Then text appeared beneath the picture:

STOP **what you're doing or next time I'll make sure no one finds you hiding in the closet.**

HER BLOOD FROZE.

If she didn't stop digging into this, he was probably going to make good with his threats.

Should she tell Jimmy James?

Probably. But she'd wait until morning.

In the meantime, she'd be lucky to get any sleep at all.

CHAPTER TWENTY

JIMMY JAMES HEADED toward Myrtle Beach the next morning. It would be about a two and a half to three-hour trip, but at least the weather was cooperating.

As he cruised through the water, he checked and saw all the controls looked good. Then he called Chief Chambers again.

The two of them were starting to feel like best friends.

After talking to Axel last night, he'd decided he needed to talk to the police chief.

"Jimmy James, what's going on?" she answered.

He swallowed hard before launching into Kenzie's theory about Ashley Nelson. After everything he'd learned, he figured it was worth the risk.

When he finished, he paused and waited for

Chief Chambers' reaction. He knew how outlandish this sounded.

"Jimmy James, you've got to know there are a lot of missing people out there," she finally said. "I don't really understand what makes this Ashley Nelson woman stand out."

He stared out over the peaceful water in front of him. "We're trying to figure that out also, and I can't give you a good answer for that. Kenzie said it's just gut instinct."

"I can appreciate that, but I can't launch an investigation into this out of pure gut instinct."

He frowned, although her reaction wasn't unexpected. "I understand, and I can't blame you for that. But I thought it was worth mentioning."

"You did the right thing by telling me. I tell you what. I'll look into the woman and see if I can find if she has any connections to this area."

His pulse slowed just slightly at knowing Chief Chambers would be investigating. "I appreciate you doing that. I know that all of this is very much out of the ordinary."

"It is. It's hard to prove a crime when you have no body and no evidence that anything happened."

"There's one other thing." Jimmy James paused a moment before telling her about the man he had Axel research.

"You and Kenzie certainly are putting a lot of

time into this." Concern stretched through the chief's voice. "That worries me."

"I know, I know. We're not trying to overstep. We just want some answers. I don't think Kenzie is going to have any peace until she does."

"That's understandable." She sighed before asking, "What makes you think this guy Axel looked into has anything to do with it?"

"I just know he's a bodyguard with a shady past and that he might be someone worth keeping an eye on."

"I appreciate your help. But you let me concentrate on this investigation, okay?"

"Yes, ma'am."

"Have a good trip, and we'll see you back in Lantern Beach tomorrow night, right?"

"That's right. I will see you then." Now he only hoped that she was able to find some answers.

KENZIE HAD JUST FINISHED CLEANING up breakfast when her phone rang. She frowned when she looked at the screen.

It was another unknown number.

Was yesterday's texter sending her another photo?

Her heart pounded harder.

She didn't think so. The area code was different. In fact . . . this looked like the area code she'd called when she had reached out to Merilee.

She glanced in the game room, where all the guests laughed over a game of ping-pong. Maybe she had a few minutes to answer without anyone scrutinizing what she was doing.

She slipped onto the deck, away from anyone who might be listening. "Kenzie Anderson."

"Kenzie, my name is Dan Jessops. I'm a reporter with *Indiana Times*."

Her heart rate quickened. Why would a reporter from Indiana be calling her? "What can I do for you?"

"I spoke with Merilee Foreman earlier today, and she mentioned a conversation she had with you. Said you suspected Ashley Nelson might be in North Carolina."

Panic raced through Kenzie. If her theory got attention, then she would be even more of a target. She had to squash his questions before he took this too far.

"I didn't say that," Kenzie told him. "I just thought I might have seen someone who looked similar to her here, and I was curious."

"She mentioned something about a man named Thatcher Davenport?"

Kenzie's panic continued to bubble until she felt

as if she couldn't breathe. She glanced around and saw everyone still seemed occupied in the game room. Despite that, she slipped farther away.

"I wasn't trying to name any names," she told him quietly. "Really. I have no evidence of any connection. I was simply asking questions."

"We're running a story on Ashley's disappearance, and I'm trying to track down any leads. Are you sure you don't know anything?"

More panic gurgled up inside her as she thought about how this might play out. None of the scenarios ended well. "No, I don't know anything. I promise. I'd really like this to not go beyond our conversation. I don't want to call out someone who could be innocent."

"If you think of anything else, let me know." He sounded unconvinced and eager for answers—answers that may or may not be there.

Kenzie noticed he didn't promise that he wouldn't run this.

She lowered her head, feeling despair nipping at her spirit.

Why had she opened her mouth last night? Why couldn't she just let this go?

She didn't know, but it was too late to do anything about it now.

CHAPTER TWENTY-ONE

JIMMY JAMES HEARD a knock at his door and called, "Come in."

Kenzie stepped inside.

He'd been hoping that the two of them would have a chance to talk, but the morning had been busy so far. Not much longer and they would pull into Myrtle Beach.

"I just wanted to let you know that I received a photo of myself last night. It was taken by someone when we were in Wilmington and sent to me along with a threat."

"What?"

She nodded, her face somber. "It's true. Someone was watching me. I thought I sensed someone, but I wrote it off. Clearly, whoever is behind this woman's murder knows who I am. He's desperate to make sure I don't talk."

"Can I see it?"

She held up her phone and let him see the photo and threatening text beneath it.

As Jimmy James stared at it, he frowned, fisting and unfisting his hands.

When he got his emotions under control, he finally said. "I don't like this."

"I know. I don't like it either."

More than anything, Jimmy James wanted to reach out to her. To pull her into his arms and tell her that everything would be okay.

His heart leapt into his throat at the thought. He couldn't do that no matter how much he wanted to.

Before they could talk any more, his phone rang, and he glanced at the screen.

It was Mr. Robertson. "I need to take this."

"Of course."

"We can talk more later, okay?"

She nodded. "Okay."

The only comfort he found was in the fact that Kenzie was onboard this boat. Last time they'd been on a charter, this boat felt almost like a prison since he wasn't sure whether one of the crew might be involved in a series of crimes.

But, right now, this boat was like a safe haven.

He prayed it stayed that way.

AS SOON AS Kenzie stepped through the door, Jimmy James put his phone to his ear. "Hello, Mr. Robertson."

"Captain Gamble. How is everything going?"

Jimmy James thought about the murder and everything else suspicious that had happened before answering with a simple, "It's going just fine."

What else was he supposed to say? Those other things didn't pertain to *Almost Paradise*. At least, he hoped they didn't.

"Good. I hoped I'd get a good report. Listen, I wanted to let you know that we have another charter guest lined up to leave the evening after you guys get back."

He sucked in a breath. "Really? That's a quick turnaround. The crew is barely going to have time to clean the boat."

"I didn't mention it earlier on purpose," Mr. Robertson said. "Our primary guest wants to keep this private."

Jimmy James was intrigued now. "Is that right?"

"Anyway, I wanted to know if you'd like to captain the next charter also. You seem to be doing a good job. I know I was dragging my feet, but I think you've earned a place on *Almost Paradise*."

Warmth spread through Jimmy James' chest at the man's words. "I appreciate that."

"So, you'll do it?"

"I would be honored."

"Great news. Now, between you and me, our next guest is . . ."

Jimmy James felt his lungs freeze with anticipation. He was anxious to hear what the big secret was.

He just hoped this secret didn't bring trouble with it.

CHAPTER TWENTY-TWO

KURT and his group requested a helicopter ride in Myrtle Beach and then they wanted to attend an outdoor concert on the beach by musical artist Bree Jordan.

Just as in Wilmington, Kenzie was part of the crew accompanying the group. Her job was mostly to keep an eye on things and make sure everyone was safe. Owen had also joined her as well as Jimmy James.

She had a feeling that the only reason Jimmy James had come along was because he wanted to keep an eye on her.

Kenzie wasn't really complaining, not considering everything that had happened.

After the flight, they arranged transportation for their party to get to the concert, which took place on a stage near the beach. It was standing room only, and the music could be heard for what felt like miles around.

Thirty minutes into the concert, Kenzie paced away from the crowd toward the edge of the group. Large groups of people were never her thing, and she fought the feeling of being overwhelmed as she'd stood among concertgoers.

While she stood in the back, one of the guests—Susan, Kurt's wife—emerged from the crowd, her hands at her temples as if she didn't feel well.

Kenzie rushed toward her. "Are you okay?"

"I'm just a little dizzy."

"Let's get you over here where you can get some fresh air." Kenzie led Susan to a nearby restaurant and let her lean against the wall.

"I think I was having a little too much fun." Susan fanned her face.

"Just take some deep breaths and stay still for a moment. Here's some water." She pulled a bottle from the backpack she carried, along with a granola bar. "Do you want me to call for medical help?"

Susan quickly shook her head and took a bite of the bar. "Oh, no. I'm sure it's just low blood sugar. Give me a minute . . ."

Kenzie waited, keeping an eye on the woman. Her medical training floated through her mind.

Susan was probably right. It sounded like hypo-glycemia.

Susan finished the bar, tossed the wrapper in the trash, then took a long sip of water. "I'm as good as new now."

Kenzie patted her back. "Are you sure?"

"Positive. Now, I think I'll go rejoin my family. Thank you for your help."

Kenzie nodded and watched her walk away. As Susan slipped back into the throng, Kenzie let out a deep breath. She was glad it was nothing more serious.

She turned to find the rest of the crew when a large group of rowdy college students left the concert area and headed toward Kenzie. She tried to step back but it was too late. She got caught up in the bustle.

The breath left her lungs as a round of panic tried to fill her.

The next moment, she felt a hand grip her arm. Before she realized what was happening, someone grabbed both her arms and shoved her into a nearby alley.

Panic bubbled through her, and she tried to turn. Before she could, something pressed into her side. "Look straight ahead."

Her lungs froze at the menacing voice. The man kept pushing her until they were behind a dumpster

—and out of sight from anyone passing by. The scent of fried seafood mixed with the rancid odor of the trash.

Kenzie's stomach churned.

"Don't scream," the man muttered in her ear. "You'll regret it if you do."

Something pressed into her side again—something hard.

A gun?

Her lungs froze.

The man squeezed Kenzie's arm harder, and she held back a yelp.

Who was this?

And what was he going to do with her?

She had no idea.

But fear spread through her so quickly that all her courage seemed to dissolve into thin air.

"WHAT DO YOU WANT FROM ME?" Kenzie asked.

"You need to stop snooping around," the man growled into her ear. "Stop asking questions. Do you understand?"

Kenzie's breath caught. She was onto something. This man wouldn't be threatening her if she wasn't.

"Who are you?" she asked as the man pressed

her against the grimy brick wall, the gun still nudged into her side.

"That's none of your business. I need to know you understand what I'm saying. Because if you don't, there will be consequences."

"Don't ask any more questions." Her words came out sounding breathless. "Got it."

Crowds sounded in the background. If Kenzie yelled, would someone help her? Or would that only end up getting her killed?

She didn't know. She couldn't risk it.

Besides, the loud music would probably drown out the sound of her voice.

"This is just the start of what's going to happen to you if you keep pressing this issue," the man continued.

"What does that mean?" Kenzie's voice trembled as she asked the question.

The next instant a shock pulsed through her.

The man had tased her, she realized.

As electricity coursed through her body, Kenzie fell to the ground, her muscles useless.

She was powerless to do anything to stop this man . . . and she had no idea what he was planning next.

CHAPTER TWENTY-THREE

AS STRANDS of a catchy acoustic number drifted through the thick air, Jimmy James glanced around the concert space and the lingering crowds.

Where had Kenzie gone? Just a few minutes ago, she'd been standing at the edge of the group of concertgoers, near a restaurant in the distance. Then his phone call had distracted him, but just for a couple of minutes.

As tension crept up his neck, he tried to keep his fears at bay and not think the worst. But considering everything that had happened . . .

He pushed through the crowd, continuing to scan everyone around him for Kenzie. But there were too many people gathered here. They all butted up against each other as they sang along. Some people danced. One group even tried to crowd surf.

Jimmy James strode toward Owen, who remained on the perimeter of the group. "Have you seen Kenzie?"

"Last time I saw her she was over there talking to Susan." Owen pointed to Seabreeze Fry House, the wood-sided building located in a long line of other shops and restaurants.

It was the same area where Jimmy James had seen Kenzie.

As Jimmy James glanced over there again, she was nowhere to be seen—and neither was Susan.

"If you see her, let me know," he muttered.

"Will do."

Jimmy James strode toward the building. He pushed by people singing along with the music, seeming as if they didn't have a care in the world. A moment of envy shot through him. But this wasn't the time to think about that now.

He reached the restaurant, the scent of fried seafood becoming stronger. The crowds were thinner here, but a lot of people still milled around—some waiting for a table and others listening to the music.

Where would Kenzie have gone? It wasn't like her to wander away.

Jimmy James paced the sidewalk, studying everyone around him in hopes of finding her. A bad feeling welled in his gut.

As he glanced down the alley running beside the restaurant, his breath caught.

Legs stuck out from behind a dumpster. He rushed toward the figure and saw a woman lying on the ground, her body as limp as a ragdoll.

"Kenzie?" The word sounded breathless as it left his lips.

Concern ricocheted through him as he rushed toward her.

More details came into focus as he got closer. Namely the red top and the khaki shorts the woman wore.

It was *definitely* Kenzie.

He knelt beside her, desperate to know if she was okay. That she was . . . alive.

"Kenzie . . ." He rolled her onto her back, praying he'd see life in her eyes.

She stared at him a moment before finally blinking.

She was alive! Relief washed through him.

Jimmy James quickly scanned her for any wounds. He saw none.

"What happened?" He lifted her shoulders against his legs and brushed her hair out of her face as he stared at her, desperate to hear confirmation that everything was okay.

She opened her mouth, but no words came out.

As more concern ricocheted through him, he reached for his phone. He needed to call 911.

But before he could hit the first number, Kenzie's hand covered his arm.

"Tasered," she muttered, the word barely discernible.

Everything clicked in his mind.

Kenzie had been tased. Of course. Everything suddenly made sense.

At once, Jimmy James' concern turned to anger.

He glanced around the alley. Where was the person who'd done this? No one was close—not even the people waiting for tables at the restaurant.

He shifted. "We need to get you to a hospital."

Kenzie squeezed his hand again and shook her head. "No . . . I'm . . . okay."

He had his doubts about that. What he wanted was to look for the person responsible for this and give him a piece of his mind. But Jimmy James didn't dare leave Kenzie.

This incident definitely confirmed that something was going on here. There was no reason for anyone to go after Kenzie unless they were trying to cover up something.

Cover up something like a murder.

SLOWLY, Kenzie felt herself regaining control of her muscles. She was so thankful that Jimmy James had shown up when he did. Just seeing him helped her to know that everything was going to be okay.

But the last thing she wanted was to make a big deal of this by going to the hospital and drawing unnecessary attention to herself. Too many questions would be asked. Too much time would be wasted.

Finally, as strands of "Living on Island Time" drifted through the air, Kenzie sat all the way up—with Jimmy James' help. But her arms and legs still trembled. She wasn't sure if it was from the taser or from nerves over what had happened.

For a moment, she'd been certain she was going to die.

Another shudder claimed her.

"Can you tell me who did this to you?" Jimmy James murmured in her ear, his thick hands brushing her hair back.

She shook her head and tried to form the right words. Losing control of her body made her head spin, made her realize just how vulnerable she really was.

"I didn't see his face." Her voice sounded strange, even to her own ears. "He approached me from behind. He had a gun. At least, I thought it was a gun. I guess it was just a taser."

"What did he say? What did he do?" Jimmy James' voice sounded hard and protective, just as she'd expected.

Thank God, he'd found her. Even with everything that had transpired between them, he still had her back, didn't he? She'd count her blessings for that.

"The man who did this. . . he just told me to stay out of his way or there would be consequences. That this was just the start."

She glanced back at Jimmy James and saw his eyes harden. He didn't like what had happened, and rightfully so. This whole situation . . . it was a mess. A mess she'd never intended to be pulled into.

If she hadn't seen the woman being murdered . . . if she hadn't screamed and drawn attention to herself . . . if she hadn't gone looking for answers.

But there was no undoing any of that. It was too late. Now all of this had been set into motion.

"Did he do anything else?" Jimmy James' voice caught as he asked the question.

Kenzie shook her head, wanting to quickly reassure him. "He just told me what he wanted me to hear, tased me, and left me here. But that was all."

Visible relief washed through Jimmy James' gaze. "We should file a police report."

She ran a hand over her face. This was such a nightmare. All of it. Today's events almost seemed surreal . . . but they weren't. "I just want to forget this happened."

"I know you do," Jimmy James murmured. "But it's best if the police have this incident on record, just in case. Plus, considering what happened . . . this is proof that you did see something happen back in Lantern Beach. You realize that, don't you?"

It took a moment for his words to settle on Kenzie before she nodded. "You're right. That man wouldn't have come after me unless I was a threat. I guess I could talk to the police just in case it makes a difference."

"I think it's a good idea." Jimmy James stood before offering his hands.

Kenzie slipped her fingers into his, and he helped her to her feet. As he did, they stood face-to-face. Close. Probably too close.

Close enough that their gazes locked and that unseen connection that stretched between them seemed to draw them closer.

She blinked, returning to her senses, and backed away.

Jimmy James had ended things. She couldn't forget that, no matter how sweet he might act.

She took a step away but wobbled. Jimmy James instantly reached for her, grabbing her elbow to keep her steady.

"I'm fine," she insisted, hating the fact that a big

deal was being made over her.

"I'm glad. But things could've turned out a lot different." He didn't let go of her—and she doubted he would.

The weight of his words settled on her. He was right. That man could have killed her tonight, and then she wouldn't be here right now talking to Jimmy James or listening to Bree Jordan's songs in the distance.

Jimmy James nodded to the street peeking from the narrow slit between buildings framing the alley. "I saw a police station not far from here. I'll walk you there so you can file your report, and I'll stay with you."

"But what about our guests?" Kurt and his group should have first priority. What if they're ready to leave? What if they noticed two members of the crew had disappeared?

She didn't want this to reflect poorly on the crew.

Jimmy James glanced at his watch. "This concert still has another hour. I'll let Owen know, but everything should be fine. And if it's not . . . I'll make sure that it's okay."

His words left no room for doubt.

He slipped his arm around her as they walked back toward the sidewalk.

Kenzie didn't complain. Right now, she desperately needed someone to help hold her up.

CHAPTER TWENTY-FOUR

JIMMY JAMES STOOD beside Kenzie as she gave her report to the police. At least that was over with now.

He had little hope the police would find the person who did this to her. No doubt, he was long gone. But the cop she'd spoken with did promise to check nearby cameras to see if those security feeds had picked up on anything.

Maybe—just maybe—they'd see something there and be able to move forward with this case. Whoever had done this to Kenzie shouldn't get away with it.

Exactly forty-five minutes after she arrived at the station, they'd been able to leave.

As Jimmy James stepped outside with Kenzie, he

glanced around the tourist-filled street, looking for any signs of trouble. He saw nothing.

But if he found the guy who did this to her . . . Anger boiled inside him.

Keep yourself in check, Jimmy James.

He knew his mental reminder was a good one. Yet he couldn't stomach the thought of someone thinking they could get away with hurting Kenzie. The notion went against everything in him.

Kenzie paused on the sidewalk and looked up at him, gratitude showing in her gaze. "Thank you for all your help."

"Of course. I'm just glad I found you when I did."

She offered a soft smile. "Me too."

He guided her back to the crew, keeping a hand on her elbow. He didn't want to let go of her—ever. Not after what had just happened.

As they strolled down the sidewalk, his thoughts clashed inside him. He needed to tell Kenzie something else. But part of him dreaded doing so. She already had a lot on her shoulders.

But he shouldn't put this off any longer. It would only make matters worse.

"Kenzie." He paused on the sidewalk and turned to her.

Her eyes widened as she looked up at him. "Yes?"

He swallowed hard before starting. "I got a call

from Mr. Robertson earlier. He wanted to talk to me about the next charter."

"Okay . . ." A knot of confusion formed between her eyes as she waited for him to continue.

"It turns out that our next guest is . . . Senator Luke Williams."

She gaped. "What?"

Jimmy James nodded. "This can't be a coincidence. I don't know what to do."

She shook her head as if trying to jostle her thoughts into place. "Just because you're the captain, that doesn't mean that you get to choose your guests."

"I know. Mr. Robertson makes those calls. I'd already agreed to captain the charter when he told me who was coming onboard."

Kenzie rubbed her arms as if chilled—even though the evening was boiling hot—before shaking her head. "I can't believe this."

"I don't blame you if you don't want to work this next charter." Part of him—a big part of him—hoped that she would stay clear.

"I can't *not* go on the charter. It's not like Mr. Robertson is going to hold my position for me if I decide to take off for a few days."

Maybe that would be the very best thing for her, though. She'd found nothing but trouble ever since she started this job.

"Kenzie—"

"Besides," Kenzie continued, not seeming to hear him. "I don't have anything else lined up. Maybe I could stay with Cassidy and Ty again. But I know they have another retreat starting soon, so there are no guarantees they'll have space for me. Besides, this is my job. It's what I signed up to do."

He licked his lips, trying to broach the subject carefully. Almost hesitantly, he asked, "Should you continue doing your job if it puts you in danger?"

Surprise filled her gaze. "We don't know for sure that the senator is going to bring danger with him. There are so many moving pieces, so many unanswered questions."

"That's the truth. But, still, I don't think it's a good idea—" Before he could finish his statement, his radio beeped.

Their guests were ready to head back to the boat for the evening.

Jimmy James frowned as they listened to the update.

He and Kenzie would talk about this again later. One way or another.

BACK AT *ALMOST PARADISE*, Kenzie performed her duties to get the boat in order before pausing to catch her breath.

She wandered to the railing on the aft deck and deeply inhaled the fresh air around her.

Glancing behind her, she saw that no one was around so she pulled out her phone. One of her father's friends, a man named Frank Weathersby, was an attorney up in the DC area and seemed knowledgeable about the political scene.

After a moment of hesitancy, Kenzie dialed his number.

He answered on the fourth ring.

Kenzie's throat tightened before she dove in. "Hi, Frank. It's Kenzie."

"Kenzie." His voice warmed. "Good to hear from you. Is everything okay?"

He and her father were the type of friends who spoke once a month or so. She doubted Frank knew she was working as a yachtie or about the tension between her and her dad. "Everything's fine. I actually had a question that I hoped you could answer. Is this a bad time?"

"I've got time for you whenever you need. What do you want to know?" His jovial voice reassured her.

"Do you know anything about a lawyer named

Thatcher Davenport from down in the Raleigh area of North Carolina?"

"Thatcher Davenport? The name is familiar." He let out a long breath. "You know what? I have heard about him. He's pretty active in the political scene, from what I remember."

"Anything else that you can recall about him?"

Frank let out another breath. "Off the top of my head? It's hard to say. But my impression of the man is that he's ruthless."

"How ruthless?"

"Ruthless enough that I'd stay away from him if I were you. Is he giving you trouble?"

Kenzie frowned as she tried to formulate how to answer that question. "I've just had a couple of run-ins with him."

"I understand. Where are you now?"

"I'm in North Carolina."

"Ah . . . it makes sense now. I heard the political race down there is brutal this year. And if Thatcher Davenport has anything to do with it, I'd stay far away."

Her gut twisted, even though she already knew his words were true without his reminder. "I'll try. Thank you for answering my questions."

"How are your dad and Leesa doing? I need to give them a call soon."

Kenzie remembered the last terse conversation

she had with her father. There was no need to go into that with Frank. "I think they're doing fine, and I'm sure he'd love to hear from you."

"You take care of yourself, Kenzie. Okay?"

"Will do." Just as she ended the call, footsteps sounded behind her.

Kenzie turned and saw Chief Stew Sunni approaching. Kenzie wasn't sure if the woman would fuss at her for taking a break or be chill. The two of them had a rocky start to their working relationship before forming a tentative friendship.

"I heard about what happened tonight," Sunni started. "Are you okay?"

Kenzie nibbled on the inside of her lip for a minute unsure about how much she wanted to say. She didn't want to draw any unnecessary attention to herself, for more than one reason.

She finally said, "I'm doing as well as can be expected. Still shaken, but I'll recover."

"Did that man who did that to you . . . did he even say what he wanted?"

"Not really. Thankfully, Captain Gamble showed up when he did."

Sunni rubbed her arms as if the whole incident had her shaken. "Sometimes as a yachtie you can deal with some real entitled jerks. I'm thankful I haven't been in a situation where I felt threatened—I mean, if I'm not counting what happened on our last charter. But still . . . I have friends who've told me horror stories."

"I've heard quite a few myself." Stories about stews being hit on, about witnessing human trafficking, about the worst of human behavior. "At least you have Eddie to watch your back."

Kenzie wasn't sure what exactly Sunni's relationship with Eddie was, but the two seemed close and she'd wondered before if they were dating.

Sunni rubbed her arms again, some of her usual arrogance disappearing. "I suppose."

"You don't sound very confident."

"I like Eddie, but he's hard to get to know. We've known each other a year, but I still feel like he has walls up, you know?"

Kenzie nodded. "I do know. Relationships can be tricky—especially when you're on a boat together."

"You would know all about that, wouldn't you?" Sunni quirked an eyebrow.

"Captain Gamble and I . . . we're not together."

"But you would be if he wasn't the captain . . ."

Kenzie shrugged. "Maybe. But as long as he's my superior . . ."

"You know, I have to admit, I was wrong about Captain Gamble. I didn't like him at first. Didn't think that he deserved the title of captain. But he's done a good job, and I feel better knowing he's watching out for us."

"He's just a guy who's trying to overcome his past. You can't fault somebody for that."

"No, I suppose you can't." Sunni pressed her lips together as she stared at the water. "Listen, I have a weird question."

Kenzie braced herself for whatever it might be. "Okay . . ."

"I saw you looking at a picture of someone on your phone. I didn't mean to snoop, but you're on the bottom bunk, and I happened to look down when you were staring at your screen."

Kenzie's heart pounded harder as she wondered where Sunni was going with this. "Okay . . ."

"The woman in the photo—the one with the long dark hair?"

Kenzie nodded. She had to be talking about Ashley Nelson. "Yes?"

"I saw her at the campground where Eddie, Owen, and I are staying."

Suddenly, Kenzie didn't notice anything else around her. The only thing that mattered was this conversation. "Is that right? What was she doing?"

"She was staying in one of the cabins, actually. She seemed awfully jumpy, which is one of the only reasons I noticed her."

"Was she alone?"

"Mostly." Sunni shrugged. "But one night, I heard her arguing with someone."

"Who? About what?"

"I couldn't make out what they were saying. But it was a woman, someone I've never seen before."

"Could you describe her?"

"I'm not sure. I think if I saw her, I could point her out, though."

"Interesting. Thank you for sharing."

Sunni nodded. "Of course. I just thought I should mention it, just in case, you know?"

"I do know. Thanks again."

Sunni let out a long breath and looked back over the water. "The good news is that this charter's gone off without too many hitches—at least so far."

"Yes, it has. Much better than our last one, huh?"

The two exchanged a look.

Kenzie straightened, knowing she couldn't stand here too long. "Well, I guess I should get back in and finish cleaning before my shift ends."

She also needed to tell Cassidy this update.

"Probably a good idea," Sunni said. "I'm glad you're okay, Kenzie."

Kenzie offered a grateful smile. "Thanks. Me too."

CHAPTER TWENTY-FIVE

WHEN JIMMY JAMES went to bed that evening, his chest felt heavy and burdened after everything that had happened—and everything he knew was coming. He turned over in bed as he tried to sort his thoughts.

In the morning, *Almost Paradise* would depart from South Carolina and head north back to Lantern Beach. There would be approximately one day to get the yacht cleaned up before their new guests joined them.

Part of him wanted to convince Kenzie to sit this next charter out. But Jimmy James understood where she was coming from when she said she wanted to stay. People were counting on her—but her life and well-being were far more important than a job responsibility. However, he didn't think he could convince her of that.

When he'd gotten back to the boat this evening, he'd called Chief Chambers and let her know what had happened in Myrtle Beach. He only wished there were more answers to offer her.

He punched his pillow beneath his head.

Had it been a mistake to end things between him and Kenzie? That's what his heart told him.

Yet he'd spoken the truth. Kenzie would be better off without someone like him. He didn't want her future to be filled with hardship just because she'd chosen to have him in her life.

And that's what would happen. Aside from the financial aspects of his future, he knew that Dr. Anderson would make Kenzie's life miserable if Jimmy James and Kenzie stayed together. Jimmy James didn't want to be the reason she and her father were divided.

Plus . . . it was like Tom said. Kenzie was pure and innocent. Jimmy James wasn't. Bad company could corrupt good character. Even though he'd changed, his history would always remain.

And his history was bad news.

He sighed and turned over in his bed again.

He had hoped he could get some sleep tonight. But he had a feeling he wouldn't.

Instead of fighting it, he stood and got dressed.

Owen had night shift this evening. But Jimmy James would join him.

After everything that had happened, having two sets of eyes on this yacht seemed like a good idea.

THE NEXT MORNING, Kenzie went through the motions of doing her job—even if she felt robotic. She set the table for breakfast, served the guests their food, and then cleaned up. She did some last-minute laundry, collected trash, and cleaned finger-prints from the windows.

Later today they would arrive back at the harbor.

In the meantime, the guests were enjoying time in the hot tub as well as in the game room on the journey back to Lantern Beach.

As she gathered some drinks to serve Kurt in the hot tub, she heard a splash and froze.

A splash.

What was that?

She paused by the railing and saw the wind had kicked up and blown a chair into the water.

But that wasn't what concerned her.

She'd heard a splash.

Because that's what happened when an object hit liquid.

Except she hadn't heard a splash on the night Ashley was killed.

She closed her eyes and pictured the scene again.

No, she was certain there hadn't been a splash.

But how was that possible?

"I'll take that drink now!" Kurt called to her.

She forced a smile as she carried the glass to him. But her mind remained on her realization.

How had she let that detail slip by? She wasn't sure. But it was significant. It had to be.

The rest of the day passed quickly as they traveled north.

Finally, they neared Lantern Beach. Seeing it was both a relief and anxiety inducing.

But as soon as the harbor came into view, Kenzie paused to stare at it.

Several police cars congregated at the back of the docks.

What exactly was going on now?

And did it have anything to do with the murder she'd seen earlier?

CHAPTER TWENTY-SIX

MORE THAN ANYTHING, Kenzie wanted to head down to the docks and see what was happening with all the police cars. But she had a job to do, and she needed to make sure everything got done before she focused on anything else—no matter how difficult that would be right now.

After docking and carrying the guests' luggage off, the crew lined up on the dock for the guests' departure. A few minutes later, their guests headed off the boat and everyone said goodbye.

Kurt handed them an envelope full of cash before telling them what an enjoyable time he'd had.

As Jimmy James held the tip in his hands, Kenzie again glanced down the docks at the scene there and frowned. Whatever was going on, it was bad. That was the only reason there would be so many police cars there.

"Let's head up to the salon for the tip meeting." Jimmy James' voice pulled her from her thoughts.

Kenzie looked away from the scene and back at Jimmy James, knowing her job wasn't done yet. She *was* curious how much tip money they earned on this trip. Nobody got rich from doing this work, but any extra money was always appreciated—especially when living on a tight budget.

But her curiosity was burning, to say the least.

With one more glance down the docks, Kenzie started toward the gangplank to *Almost Paradise*. As she did, she paused.

A woman standing in the parking lot caught her eye.

Was that . . . ?

Kenzie's breath caught. It was.

Thatcher Davenport's wife was here. On Lantern Beach.

The woman was slightly hard to recognize in a floppy hat and sunglasses, but Kenzie knew without a doubt that's who it was. Her curly blonde hair protruded from beneath her hat, and her form-fitting leopard print dress showed off her curva-ceousness.

As Sunni began to walk past, Kenzie touched her arm to stop her.

Kenzie waited until everyone else had passed by before she asked Sunni a question. "Do you see that woman over there?"

Sunni followed her gaze. "I do."

"Was that the person you saw arguing at the campground with the woman in the photo you saw on my phone?"

She squinted before shaking her head. "No, she's not."

"You're sure?"

"I'm positive. The woman I saw wasn't as curvy. Her hair was smoother."

Kenzie frowned.

She thought she might have a lead, but apparently not.

Still . . . when had Thatcher's wife arrived on the island?

AS SOON AS Jimmy James finished with the tip meeting, he strode down the dock toward the police cars. Several boats were moored near them—including *Seas the Day*.

He frowned. That meant Thatcher was still here, along with his dishonorably discharged bodyguard. The two of them were at the top of his list of potential suspects behind everything that had happened

—including the dead woman and even Kenzie's taser incident.

Even if the boat remained here, someone affiliated with it could have driven down to Myrtle Beach to deliver their threatening message to Kenzie.

"Hey, wait!" someone said behind him.

He paused on the dock and glanced back in time to see Kenzie jogging toward him. He'd tried to slip away without her. But he should have known better. Should have known that she would want to see what was going on down here also, especially since it concerned her.

"What do you think happened?" she asked as she caught up with him.

He glanced at the scene and shrugged. "I have no idea. But with all this commotion, it's probably something big."

Quietly, they walked together until pausing beside the police cars parked at the edge of the scene.

They arrived just in time to see a crane lifting something covered in a tarp from the water. Slowly, the machine swiveled and set the tarp-encased object on the docks. As one of the edges flopped open, a swollen hand emerged.

Kenzie gasped and turned to Jimmy James. The next instant, she buried her face in his chest.

Instinctively, Jimmy James' arm went around her as he continued to stare at the scene in front of him.

Based on the painted nails, that was a woman's body.

Was this the person Kenzie had seen killed aboard *Seas the Day*?

He frowned.

That was his best guess.

CHAPTER TWENTY-SEVEN

KENZIE COULDN'T BELIEVE what she was seeing.

A body had been lifted from the water.

A woman's body.

Everything clicked in her mind. This *had* to be the person she'd seen being shoved off the boat after being strangled.

This was the evidence they'd been looking for.

But perhaps part of her had hoped the whole thing was just her imagination. That someone hadn't died.

That didn't seem possible right now.

If she was right, when the police identified this body, they'd discover it was Ashley Nelson.

Jimmy James kept an arm around her, and she appreciated his strength as he held her steady on her feet right now. Her knees felt weak as she observed the scene.

She continued to watch as law enforcement surrounded the body.

Several minutes later, Chief Chambers rose and made her way toward them, a grim look on her face. "It looks like you got back just in time."

"Is that her?" Kenzie rushed, unable to hold back her question.

Cassidy hesitated a moment before shrugging. "It's too early to say."

"But if you had to guess?" Jimmy James asked.

Chief Chambers hesitated another moment before nodding. "I have a feeling this ties in with what you saw a few nights ago."

"How did you find her?" Kenzie glanced behind the chief to where *Seas the Day* was docked.

This boat slip was at least ten down.

"There was a chain wrapped around this woman's ankle. Most likely, a weight of some sort had been attached to it that would ensure her body sank. But something happened and the chain broke free. She floated to the surface, and a fisherman found her this morning."

Kenzie let out a little gasp, and, as she did, Jimmy James pulled her close again.

"Are you both going to be around for a couple more hours?" Chief Chambers asked.

"We are," Jimmy James answered.

"Good." Chief Chambers' grim look spoke volumes. "Because I might have a few more questions for you."

"I HAVE a bad feeling in my gut," Jimmy James told Kenzie as they remained on the dock.

At his words, Kenzie's hand went to her stomach. She felt unsettled too, to say the least. "Me also. Yet in another way I feel a little justified. Maybe now people will realize that I wasn't going crazy."

"I never thought that you were crazy."

"But you might be the only one."

"I'm just afraid that whatever you saw has pulled you into some type of scheme that you never wanted to be a part of. Last night proved it when that man tasered you in the alley."

She visibly shivered beside him. "I made a mistake."

"What?"

She licked her lips and nodded. "I called one of Ashley's friends and asked questions. This friend gave my number to a reporter who wanted to follow up. I told him I didn't know anything. But if this guy started asking questions . . . then it may have made the killer feel more threatened. That might be why he came after me yesterday."

"Kenzie . . ."

She raised her hand. "I know. It was stupid. But I can't change it. The question is, what do I do about it now?"

"I could give you some money." His eyes lit with hope. "You could leave. Go somewhere else where you'll be safe."

Kenzie paused and looked up at him. "You would do that for me?"

"I don't want to see you get hurt." His voice cracked as he said the words.

She started to reach for him but stopped herself. "Thank you, Jimmy James."

His throat went dry. More than anything, he wanted to pull her toward him. To wrap her in his arms. To tell her how much she had come to mean to him.

But he couldn't do that—for so many reasons.

"I'm not letting this deter me from my plans," she finally announced. "Too many people have tried to control my life. And I'm done with it. From now on, I'm calling the shots."

Even though her words didn't surprise him, Jimmy James frowned.

But he had to wonder if she was referring to him

also when she talked about people who tried to make decisions for her.

CHAPTER TWENTY-EIGHT

EACH TASK HAD BEEN DIVVIED up among the crew for the upcoming trip. They'd all been hard at work since their return that afternoon.

However, because of the quick turnover, their provisions hadn't yet been delivered, and they needed food before they hit the open seas again.

Chef Durango was going to head to the grocery store in town, but he needed someone to go with him. Everything wouldn't fit in his car.

"I'll go," Kenzie volunteered.

"Perfect," Durango said. "Let me go grab my car keys, and I'll meet you in five. Sound good?"

"That works."

Kenzie noticed that Jimmy James still stood there, even after Durango left. She knew exactly what he was thinking. He was worried.

"I'll be fine," she insisted. "I'll walk to my car with Durango and won't do anything risky."

He stared at her, still hesitant. "I worry about you."

"I know. But I'll be careful."

Before he could say anything else, Durango appeared. "Ready to go? Time is wasting."

Kenzie pulled her gaze away from Jimmy James' and nodded. "Let's hit the road."

It would be good to get off the boat for a while. She needed to sort out her thoughts about so many things, not just including the murder she'd seen. She also needed to figure out things with Jimmy James.

It was so hard being around him knowing that he didn't want the two of them to be together. Or he wouldn't *allow* them to be together.

She and Durango walked quietly from *Almost Paradise* toward the parking lot. It was getting dark outside, but just enough sunlight remained. Instead of talking, Durango stared at his list and mumbled things to himself, obviously frazzled by the quick turnaround.

That was fine by her.

Her thoughts continued to turn over as well.

Part of Kenzie felt angry at Jimmy James' decision to call things off between them, so angry that she wanted nothing to do with him. But whenever she was around Jimmy James, she remembered his kind spirit and her heart wanted what her heart wanted.

They paused by Kenzie's car.

"Here we are," Durango said. "You good now?"

She swirled her keys around her finger. "I'm good. I'll meet you at the grocery store."

"Yes, let's do that. We don't have any time to waste."

She climbed into her Corolla, inhaling a deep breath and flashing a reassuring smile at Durango. As soon as he disappeared, her grin faded.

Maybe she could finally breathe for a minute.

As she cranked her engine, she heard something shift behind her. Before she could turn and identify the sound, something hard pressed into her side.

A shadow appeared in the backseat and said, "If you scream, I'll shoot you."

———

JIMMY JAMES LEFT the boat to talk to Stevie-o about gassing up.

When he walked into the marina office, he spotted his friend at the desk. Stevie-o held that envelope of money Jimmy James had seen Thatcher hand to him and was counting out the bills.

Enough was enough.

Jimmy James was tired of skirting around the truth.

It was time to be direct.

"What's going on, Stevie-o?" Jimmy James stepped closer.

As he did, Stevie-o flinched and nearly dropped his money. Instead, he quickly shoved it into the drawer and closed it. "Do you make it a habit of sneaking up on people?" The harbormaster glared at Jimmy James.

"It appeared you were so distracted you didn't even hear me step inside. I wasn't being sneaky about it."

Stevie-o crossed his arms. "What can I do for you?"

"I need to gas up. But, before I do that, why don't you tell me what's going on?"

"What are you talking about?"

He nodded toward the drawer. "Why did Thatcher give you that money?"

"Thatcher Davenport? Why do you think he gave it to me?"

"Don't play dumb with me." Jimmy James lowered his voice to a growl. "I saw the exchange the other day but backed out of the office because I thought I was interrupting something. There are too many secrets here at this harbor for my comfort, though."

Stevie-o let out a sigh before shifting his eyes. "It's complicated."

"Are you involved with that woman's murder?"

"What?" Stevie-o's eyes widened. "No! Of course not. Why would you think that?"

"I'm only telling you what it looks like—like Thatcher is guilty, and he's paying you to stay quiet."

"That's ludicrous. I would never do that."

Jimmy James crossed his thick arms over his chest. "Are you sure about that?"

Stevie-o let out a sigh and stepped closer. "Look, I did take some money from Thatcher but not for that reason."

"Then why?"

Stevie-o sighed again. "Truthfully? My wife has gotten into some spending debt, and I'm desperately trying to get us out of it. So, I took some money on the side from Thatcher."

"What did he give you money for, Stevie-o?"

Stevie-o remained silent.

"That's okay. You don't have to tell me. I'll just let Chief Chambers know and—"

"No!" Stevie-o scrubbed a hand over his face before lowering his voice. "Don't do that. Please. It's not what you think."

"Then what is it?"

"Thatcher asked me if he could use that slip while he was here."

"That precise slip?" Jimmy James clarified.

"That's right. I didn't ask any questions. I only know that someone else had it reserved. I usually don't make it a point of giving people special treatment. But Thatcher persuaded me otherwise."

"And you have no idea why?"

"No idea."

Jimmy James stared at him another moment before nodding. "You should probably tell Chief Chambers this information, just in case it's pertinent to her investigation."

"I'm afraid she'll ask too many questions."

"But if she finds out you were withholding information . . . then you'll be in a lot more trouble than just financial."

Stevie-o frowned before nodding. "You're probably right. Is that what you came to talk to me about?"

"No, I just need to gas up."

Stevie-o nodded. "I can do that."

So maybe his friend wasn't a part of what had happened. But someone who'd been here at this harbor was.

Jimmy James needed to find out who.

CHAPTER TWENTY-NINE

"WHO ARE you and what do you want from me?" Kenzie's voice trembled as she was keenly aware of the gun pressed into her.

"I'm the one who'll be talking. Do you understand?"

She said nothing, just waited for this man to continue.

"You need to do exactly what I tell you or your friend Jimmy James will go to prison."

"What do you mean?" The question escaped before she could stop it.

"I mean, we have pictures of him breaking and entering aboard *Seas the Day*. All I have to do is make one call and the police will have no excuse not to arrest him. And with his track record, he'll go to prison again."

Kenzie sucked in a breath. That man who'd locked her in the closet . . . he must have stayed close. Must have watched as Jimmy James rescued her.

Could he really go to prison for going aboard? She thought it was a real possibility.

Or what if this guy wasn't telling the truth?

"You're bluffing," she finally murmured.

"Do you want to test that theory?"

Kenzie's spine stiffened. No, she did *not* want to test that theory. Because she could very easily see how that would play out. Jimmy James would be an easy scapegoat for anything like that. Whoever was behind this knew that and was using it for leverage.

"What do you want from me?" Her voice trembled again as she asked the question.

"You have an upcoming charter with Senator Williams," the man started.

Her breath caught. Of *course,* that was what this was about.

"Since you've already inserted yourself into our business, then we're just going to let you continue to do that."

"What do you want?"

"I just want you to be friendly with him."

Her heart rate slowed to a dull thud. "What does that mean?"

"You know. *Friendly.*"

"I'm friendly to everyone."

"You need to be even more friendly with him. The kind of friendly where you touch his arm and shoulder and talk to him at night when everyone else is sleeping."

Kenzie sucked in a breath. Was this man saying that he needed to be caught in a compromising position?

That's what it sounded like to her.

"I'm not that type of person."

"We're not saying you have to do anything that goes too far. But you're his type. We just need you to be friendly, as I said earlier."

"And if I don't?"

"It's like I said, charges will be pressed against Jimmy James. He probably won't be able to keep his captain's license, and we both know he's worked so hard to get where he is. He'll be forced to work the docks until he retires—if he can even retire. I heard the pay for this job isn't great. I'm sure that's not what you want."

Kenzie's mind raced. "Even if I do what you want, how are you going to know?"

"We have people everywhere. We'll know."

She didn't say anything. Her mind raced through all the possibilities. But however she looked at it, the whole situation seemed lose-lose.

"Are we clear as to what this agreement is?" the

man finally said.

Kenzie wanted to say no. She wanted to scream and jump out of the car. But she couldn't do that. Not with the gun pressed into her side.

"Are we clear?" he asked again.

"Yes." The word sounded harsh and garbled.

"Great. I'm glad we could come to this agreement. I'm going to climb out of the car, and I want you to wait ten seconds until you pull away. Do you understand?"

"Yes."

Then she heard the door open, and the man ran away.

JIMMY JAMES COULDN'T HELP but notice that Kenzie seemed shaken as she helped carry the provisions from the car onto the yacht. The whole crew had pitched in to help. But Jimmy James kept stealing glances at Kenzie, trying to figure out what had caused the change in her.

Finally, he caught her alone in the galley. "Is everything okay?"

Kenzie cast him a quick glance before plastering on a smile and setting a box of vegetables on the counter. "Yes. Of course. Why?"

"You're not acting like yourself."

"I just have a lot to get done," she said as she walked back to the door, clearly not wanting to stop and talk. "But I'm fine."

He followed behind, trying to figure out how hard he should push. "Just checking. With everything that's happened, you never know."

"I suppose that is true."

After they finished unloading, they had a crew meeting in the salon again. Jimmy James chose not to reveal who the guests were for the charter quite yet. Because the sooner he revealed it, the more chances there were for that news to slip and for people to hear that the senator was going to be on the boat.

He didn't want to risk that. Especially since Mr. Robertson had repeatedly reminded him about how the senator wanted privacy.

"I need everyone to be here to report for duty by nine a.m. This place needs to be spic-and-span. The guests will arrive at ten, and we need to make sure we give them a vacation of a lifetime. Understand?"

Everyone around him nodded.

"Good news then. You're all free to go."

As everyone dispersed, Jimmy James saw a new figure step on the boat.

Chief Chambers.

His heart thumped in his chest as he anticipated what she might have to say.

CHAPTER THIRTY

KENZIE FELT her throat tighten when she saw
Chief Chambers step onto the boat with a grim look
on her face. What now?

Please, Lord . . . no more bad news.

Kenzie had really been hoping that she and
Jimmy James could talk. That she could get some
things off her chest—things like how she was so
tired of people trying to control her life.

First, her father.

Then, Jimmy James.

Just now, the man who'd been in her car.

Sometimes it felt like everyone tried to play her
like a pawn.

That wasn't okay. She was fully capable of
making her own choices. She had a good head on

her shoulders. She didn't make risky moves—not usually, at least.

When would she find someone who'd let her be herself? Who gave her freedom to make mistakes? Who trusted her judgment, especially when it came to Kenzie's future?

Those things were the least of her concerns right now, though.

Did Chief Chambers know about the man in her car? Had he already made good with his threat and sent those pictures to the police?

There were almost too many worst-case scenarios vying for her attention.

"I was hoping to find you here." The chief paused in front of Kenzie.

Kenzie's throat burned with dread. "Is everything okay?"

"I know you said it was dark outside when you saw the incident several nights ago. So, I realize it's a longshot that you would be able to identify the victim."

Kenzie nibbled on her bottom lip as she waited for the police chief to continue.

"But I wondered if I showed you a picture of the woman we found today if it might ring any bells with you."

"I'd be willing to try." Kenzie's heart pounded harder in her ears.

"I know that this isn't easy," Chief Chambers said. "Seeing a dead body never is."

"I'll be okay."

Chief Chambers grimaced before pulling out her phone and tapping on the screen. A moment later, she showed Kenzie a photo there.

The face was bloated and discolored.

But the dark hair . . . the skin tone . . . the age . .
.

Kenzie couldn't tell for sure, but she thought she knew who this was.

To confirm her theory, she glanced at the woman's collarbone.

She could barely make out a small lightning tattoo there.

Her breath caught as all doubt left her mind.

"It's Ashley Nelson," Kenzie said. "The student from Indiana who went missing last week."

THE REST of the crew went belowdecks to get cleaned up. But Jimmy James stayed on the main deck, trying to ready himself for his new guests.

Kenzie joined him at the railing.

He stared at her as she stood, overlooking the water. The late afternoon sun hit her glossy hair, making it shimmer and causing her skin to glow.

She was so beautiful. He'd thought that from the moment he met her.

Her long, dark hair that flowed over her shoulders. Her olive complexion. Her brown eyes. The combination took his breath away.

But it was more than her physical beauty that caught his attention. Kenzie also had a kind spirit. A vulnerability that he wasn't used to seeing. And she was smart as well.

He drew in a deep breath as he stepped closer. Maybe breaking things off with her had been a huge mistake. It was certainly his loss.

But what about Kenzie? What her father said was true. She would be better off without him. She couldn't even deny that, could she?

"You thinking about Ashley Nelson?" he finally asked.

Kenzie stared out at the water and nodded. "I can't stop thinking about her. That poor girl . . . how had she gone from being a law student in Indiana to being murdered in Lantern Beach?"

"That's a good question. I'm sure the police are working on it."

"It just seems like a nightmare."

"Yes, it does," Jimmy James said. "How are you holding up?"

She shrugged but didn't look back at him. Even her shoulders seemed slouched, as if they bore unseen burdens. "I don't know what to think anymore."

His gaze remained on her—unapologetically. "Are you ever tempted to go back to med school?"

She didn't hesitate before shaking her head as if that answer didn't require any thought. "No, I have no desire to go back to that. I guess I just have some things I need to figure out—things that don't include med school."

Was one of those things that she needed to figure out whether or not her dad's words were true?

Why was Jimmy James hoping against hope that they wouldn't be? It was ridiculous. He just needed to let this go. He needed to let Kenzie go.

Yet the woman was never far from his thoughts. He couldn't stop thinking about what their future might look like together.

Better for him. That was for sure.

But for her? That was still up in the air.

He needed to resign himself that this was his future, and Kenzie would not be a part of it.

CHAPTER THIRTY-ONE

KENZIE STARED up at Jimmy James, unable to hold back her thoughts any longer. "It shouldn't be your call, you know."

Jimmy James glanced at her as if startled. "*What* shouldn't be my call?"

"My future." She stabbed her chest with her finger.

His eyebrows shot up. "What are you talking about?"

"You're deciding for me that you wouldn't be right for my future. It's like something my dad would do, and I don't appreciate it." She crossed her arms.

"That's not fair . . ."

She felt herself springing to life. "What's not fair is *you* making a decision based on how you think *I'm* going to react. It's my call how I want to live the rest of my life."

"Kenzie . . ." Jimmy James started to reach for her, but when she stepped away, he dropped his hand.

"It's true. You listened to my dad instead of listening to me and how I told you that I felt. It's not fair. I gave up everything to come here because it was my choice to do that. And it's going to be my choice how I spend my future. Including who it's with. Where I live. What I do. Nobody else is going to make those calls for me."

Jimmy James opened his mouth to say something before straightening and nodding. "I understand. You're right. It *should* be your call. But your dad had a point. You have to admit that."

She scowled. "He didn't have a point. He just said what he did because he thinks he's the smartest person in the room. He is sometimes. But not always."

Jimmy James tilted his head, his gaze pleading with her. "Kenzie . . . answer this honestly. Could you really see yourself living here on this island with me? I have a little cottage, but it's humble. Probably a far cry from what you're used to. I don't have a lot of disposable income. My budget is tight. My reputation is tarnished. I'm not someone you're probably going to want to show off to your friends who are all wildly more successful than I'll ever be."

Kenzie gawked, unable to hold back her disbelief. "I don't know what you're talking about. You're the captain of a superyacht. You're living the life you've made for yourself here on an island off the coast of North Carolina. Do you know how many people would love to get away from everything and move to an island? Do you know how many people want to do that but they're just too afraid to take the plunge?"

"Kenzie—"

She kept going. "Material possessions . . . they can weigh a person down. It's what people think that they want, what they think makes them successful. But, in the end, possessions just end up being burdens. As does the process of obtaining them. And those things aren't important to me."

"Kenzie—"

"If you'd asked me, I would have told you that." She hadn't realized all the emotions that had been simmering inside her for quite a while.

But they had.

Kenzie had just pushed them down, distracted with everything else. This was one of the first chances that the two of them had really been able to talk one-on-one.

"I'm sorry." Jimmy James' voice trailed with sincerity. "I don't know what to say."

She shrugged and took a step back. "There's probably nothing you can say. I just needed to speak my piece. You've made your decision."

He let out a long breath and rubbed a hand over his face.

"I like you, Jimmy James. I really do. But I can never be with someone who will listen to what my father thinks is best over what I think is best."

As she walked away from Jimmy James, she drew in a deep breath, trying to regain control of her feelings.

Kenzie's emotions felt so strong that she was actually trembling.

It felt good to get things off her chest. But it was going to take some time to process all of this.

JIMMY JAMES COULDN'T STOP THINKING about the conversation he'd had with Kenzie last night.

She certainly hadn't wasted any words. And he couldn't blame her for the way she felt either. She had every right to feel that way.

But right now, it was a new day, and he had a lot

to get done. Starting with the crew meeting at nine a.m.

They all gathered in the salon, and he handed out the preference sheets. A preference sheet was given out each time they had a guest on a charter, and it detailed each person who would be aboard, along with their photo, their culinary likes and dislikes, activities they were interested in, and any other pertinent information.

As soon as the crew saw the picture of Senator Williams, he heard a murmur go around the room.

"Yes, you're reading that correctly. Senator Williams will be our guest this week, along with his wife, his two children, his campaign manager, and two bodyguards. It's very important that we keep his presence here under wraps. That's why I waited so long to tell you he was going to be aboard."

"Does this change how we are going to do anything?" Eddie asked.

"We are still going to give the top-notch service that we always give. We're just going to do everything with discretion. The senator doesn't want to make any stops. He mostly just wants to enjoy some time here on the yacht away from everyone else and any media. Do you all understand that?"

"Yes, Captain" went around the circle.

His gaze stopped at Kenzie who'd also agreed

with his statements. His heart panged when he saw her, but he pushed the feeling down.

Mostly he was just worried about any implications the senator's presence here could have on her. Was she still a target, even now that Ashley Nelson has been found? He wasn't sure.

When he finished the meeting, he glanced at the time on his watch. Senator Williams should be arriving in ten minutes. That meant they needed to get ready to line up and greet their new guests.

Jimmy James prayed that the charter went without a hitch.

For more than one reason.

CHAPTER THIRTY-TWO

KENZIE PLASTERED on a smile despite her nerves as she greeted each member of Senator Williams' party.

Senator Williams was in his forties with sparkling blue eyes, dark hair, and a winsome grin. She could see why he was elected to office because he seemed to exude friendliness and charm.

His wife, Lori, was a blonde with a short bob haircut and a more hesitant smile.

They also had two sons, Robbie and Reggie, who were nine and eleven respectively.

His campaign manager, Alexandra, also came along. The woman was everything Kenzie imagined a campaign manager to be—brisk, a fast talker, and uptight to a T.

Rounding out the group were two security

guards who offered curt nods as they'd walked down the line.

The crew grabbed all their guests' luggage and carried it onboard, while Sunni gave them a tour of the boat and let them pick out their accommodations.

As soon as the guests were settled and gathered in the main salon, Jimmy James joined them and explained that their trip would be getting underway soon. Lunch would be served in two hours on the afterdeck. Until then, they were free to explore the boat. At lunch they'd talk about their itinerary for the rest of the week.

As Jimmy James spoke to them, Kenzie's gaze kept going back to Senator Williams.

He looked earnestly happy to be on this cruise. Would she really be able to do what the man in her car had demanded?

She couldn't see herself purposefully trying to ruin someone else's life. But if she didn't do this, then someone else would purposefully try to ruin Jimmy James' life.

Neither option seemed fair.

And neither option seemed like one she could live with.

Kenzie rubbed her arms as she stared at the senator and then at Jimmy James.

What was she going to do?

LATER IN THE EVENING, Kenzie stood at the rail looking at the horizon.

"Hi, there," a soft voice said.

She glanced over and saw Lori Williams approaching.

Kenzie quickly flashed a smile. "Good evening."

Lori paused, leaning on the rail beside her. "I love it out here. It's so peaceful, and it helps me feel balanced, if that makes sense."

"I totally understand. I feel the same way." Kenzie straightened, realizing she was feeling a little too comfortable. "Can I get you something to drink?"

Lori waved her hand in the air before touching the necklace at her throat. "No, don't be ridiculous. Consider yourself off duty."

Kenzie smiled again. She liked this woman. She seemed sweet and down-to-earth—not the kind of person Kenzie would ever want to purposefully hurt. Not that she'd want to hurt anyone.

She suppressed a sigh.

"It feels so good to get away from everything," Lori continued. "You can't imagine the pressures of this political race."

"No, I can't. You seem to retain your composure well."

"It's taken a lot of practice. Believe me. I wasn't born this way. I was *shaped* this way."

Kenzie wasn't sure how to take that statement. But part of her understood being forced into a role that you weren't quite comfortable with. She'd broken away from those expectations for her life.

But this was just the start of forging her own way. It wouldn't be easy, but she hoped the payoff was worth it.

"Whatever you do, don't let anyone make you into someone you're not." Lori gripped the rail until her knuckles turned white. "Because, one day, you might wake up and realize you're just a shell of who you used to be."

Kenzie swallowed hard. "Thanks for the advice."

"You probably think I'm crazy."

"I don't. Not at all. In fact, I'm here against my family's wishes. I was supposed to go back to med school soon."

Lori's eyes lit. "Good for you, taking control of your own destiny. Color me impressed."

"Thanks for the encouragement. I doubt myself sometimes."

"Everyone else will doubt you," Lori said. "The only person you can depend on to believe in you is yourself."

Lori's words echoed in her head. It was true. She

had to believe in herself. She couldn't wait for other people to catch up.

Before they could talk anymore, a new sound rang in the darkness.

Gunfire.

Kenzie sucked in a breath before yelling, "Duck!"

Then she tackled Lori to the deck.

CHAPTER THIRTY-THREE

THE BODYGUARDS RUSHED TOWARD THEM.

Kenzie's heart pounded as she waited, anticipating the worst. Anticipating pain. Chaos.

Danger.

"It was fireworks," one of the guards said.

Kenzie felt herself freeze. "Fireworks?"

As if to answer her question, red and blue lights cascaded in the sky from the shore in the distance.

The bodyguard nodded, quickly rolling his eyes to the side as if annoyed. "That's right."

Kenzie pulled herself away from Lori and frowned as she realized she'd overreacted. "I'm so sorry, ma'am."

The guards helped Lori to her feet, and she brushed her designer pants off as she composed herself. "It's . . . okay. You really are trained well on this charter, aren't you?"

"I . . . my mind went to worst-case scenarios. I apologize again. I didn't hurt you, did I?"

"No, you didn't. I appreciate your diligence." She fluffed her hair before nodding toward the interior. "But I think I'll retire for the evening now. I've had my excitement for the night."

"Of course." Kenzie's cheeks still flushed.

As Lori departed, the two guards flanked either side of her.

Kenzie fanned her warm face, wishing she could have a redo. The fireworks still exploding in the distance almost seemed to taunt her, each explosion reminding her that she'd overreacted.

Was this what Kenzie's life had come down to? Always being nervous about what was going to happen next?

That's how it seemed.

She wasn't sure she was going to be able to move past this until whoever had killed Ashley was put behind bars.

Who could the murderer be?

Initially, she'd thought it might be Thatcher or one of his men. But they had alibis.

Could Ashley Nelson have enemies who'd followed her here?

Who was the woman Sunni had seen arguing with Ashley?

Was Harbormaster Stevie-o hiding something?

Kenzie still had so many questions and not enough answers.

JIMMY JAMES HEARD a knock on the door behind him and turned, hoping to see Kenzie step onto the bridge.

His hopes were dashed when he saw Senator Williams instead.

Jimmy James forced a smile. "Senator. How are you?"

"Hello, Captain Gamble." Senator Williams took another step inside. "Do you mind?"

"Not at all," Jimmy James said. "Come on over."

The senator came and stood beside him at the helm. "I hear your crew is very well trained."

Jimmy James frowned. He'd heard what happened with Lori Williams. He knew Kenzie was on edge after everything that happened.

But guests couldn't be tackled for no reason.

"I apologize for that," Jimmy James said.

"It's okay. It's kind of funny, actually. Maybe not to Lori but . . ." He shrugged.

Jimmy James was thankful they weren't more upset about the incident.

The senator shoved that topic aside and began asking questions, and Jimmy James explained how the boat operated.

"Let me just tell you," Senator Williams said. "It's great to be here. I look forward to getting away from the rat race, and I appreciate you accommodating us. I know that our request was last minute."

"If you don't mind me asking, how did you even hear about us?"

"Through a friend of a friend," he said. "He told me you guys were new and, because of that, had some openings. I didn't even know charters like this left from the North Carolina coast."

"I can only imagine that things are probably pretty stressful for you around this time of year with the election looming," Jimmy James said.

"You can say that again." Senator Williams stared into the water. "I love what I do, but I don't actually love campaigning. It takes away from my real work —making this country live up to her potential. To do that, you have to make compromises sometimes."

Jimmy James swallowed hard as questions circled in his head. "I imagine the scrutiny is hard."

"It is. I guess you learn that it comes with the job."

"And the threats?" Jimmy James glanced at him, hoping he wasn't overstepping. "I'm assuming you have some since you brought two bodyguards with you. Seems like it would come with the territory."

Senator Williams frowned. "Yes, there are always threats—especially from the Kinnakeet Society."

Jimmy James' breath caught. "The Kinnakeet Society?"

Senator Williams threw a surprised glance at him. "I'm surprised you haven't heard of them. It's an environmental group, and they've decided that they hate me ever since I gave my support to an oil company that wants to drill wells in the ocean."

"They're that upset, huh?"

He let out a garbled chuckle and nodded. "Yes, they are. In fact, they poured oil all over my car one day—oil, the very substance they're so opposed to. It only escalated from there."

"They sound pretty vile."

"They're passionate and vile—a very dangerous combination."

Jimmy James stored the name of that group in the back of his mind, just in case it was significant.

If someone for some reason was targeting the senator, maybe it was a member of that group.

Jimmy James couldn't say for sure that the senator was being targeted. But it seemed like too much of a coincidence for him to be here and not be in some sort of danger.

His back muscles bristled at the thought.

Just what had he gotten himself into as captain of this charter?

CHAPTER THIRTY-FOUR

THE FIRST DAY of the charter had proven, so far, to be uneventful. At least, in Kenzie's estimation.

The senator and his family had been pleasant to be around and hadn't been too demanding like some guests tended to be. Kenzie had heard stories about some guests who demanded hundreds of peach roses to adorn the space during their charter or exotic fruits shipped from other countries or expensive workout equipment.

As Kenzie headed toward the laundry, she paused when she saw the senator reading a book on one of the lounge chairs.

She glanced around but didn't see anyone else nearby. His two guards were stationed on either side of the boat, but not near the senator. Not right now, at least.

Kenzie licked her lips. Was this her chance to do something?

Her stomach turned at the thought of it. It *did* seem like a good opportunity. All she had to do was step close to him and start up a casual conversation. Maybe brush something out of his eye. Maybe pretend to stumble and have him catch her.

She didn't want to do any of those things. They weren't in her nature. In fact, thinking about the request just made her angry.

There was no way she could do this. No way.

But if she were to do it . . . then this would be the perfect time. It was like the opportunity was right in front of her.

Jimmy James' face flashed in her mind. Then she thought about him giving up everything to go to jail.

Part of her thought that it was her fault. She was the one who had caused this. As a result, now she was being targeted, as was Jimmy James because of his connection to her.

Whatever happened, it felt like it would all be her fault.

She rubbed her throat as she felt it tighten.

Maybe she should do it. Just make it something innocent and quick. She could deny it later because nothing was going to happen.

She frowned again. She just couldn't bring

herself to go any closer. Every fiber of her being rebelled at the thought of it.

"Could you get me some water?"

Kenzie startled at the sound. She looked up and saw one of the security guards standing near her.

How long had he been watching her?

She wasn't sure. The fact that she wasn't sure made her uncomfortable. She had to pay better attention.

Either way, it looked like her opportunity was now gone.

Kenzie smiled at the security guard. "Of course. One moment."

Then she disappeared into the galley to retrieve his drink.

THEY ANCHORED the boat for the evening off the coast of Beaufort, a small, historic town nestled on the North Carolina coast.

In the meantime, Jimmy James stepped onto the main deck and spotted the senator reading in a lounge chair.

Did Williams have any idea he could be in danger? Did he have any idea that the woman who'd died in Lantern Beach harbor was somehow connected with the man running against him for office?

His gaze went to the security guards flanking either side of him.

Something about their presence on the boat bothered Jimmy James. Maybe it was their aloofness. The secret looks they exchanged. The way they acted as if they were the top authority on the boat.

Feeling satisfied for the moment that everything was okay, he headed back to the captain's quarters.

After grabbing his computer, he looked up that environmental group that the senator had told him about earlier.

Kinnakeet Society.

He scrolled through pages of things they'd objected to. Many of their protests were centered along the North Carolina coast.

And they were *very* vocal about their opposition.

They had a distinct symbol—a circle with waves at the bottom and a silhouette of a pelican above it.

He'd seen that somewhere before.

Where?

Jimmy James couldn't place it, but he thought for sure it was a sticker he'd seen on a car at the harbor recently.

Was that significant?

He wasn't sure, but it could be.

Next, he went to Ashley Nelson's page on social

media and began to scroll through all her posts. He didn't expect to find anything.

But he saw a post from a year ago.

A post that was shared from the Kinnakeet Society.

Ashley had clearly been aware of who they were. Was this group the connection he'd been looking for? Was Sampson somehow tied in with this whole mess also?

There were too many pieces that didn't connect . . . Not yet.

But if Jimmy James wanted Kenzie safe, then he needed to figure out how all these people were connected. Maybe when he saw where the lines intersected, he'd have his answer about what had really happened.

CHAPTER THIRTY-FIVE

KENZIE STILL FELT uneasy as she grabbed a quick turkey and cheese sandwich in the crew mess. It was late, but she hadn't eaten yet, and their guests—minus the children who'd gone to bed—were still going strong. That meant she couldn't end her shift yet.

She knew she'd made the right decision earlier. She wouldn't be able to set up any type of incriminating photos of herself with the senator. She couldn't do it. Ever. For any reason.

But she needed to figure out a way to also help Jimmy James in the process. She just didn't know what that was.

She took another bite of her sandwich as she sat at the small, cramped table. The only way she'd be able to truly help him was to figure out who was behind this. Who was the man in her car?

Clearly, someone was in great opposition to Senator Williams. That person would do whatever it took to make sure Williams didn't get reelected.

Did this also tie in with the murder of Ashley Nelson? It was the only thing that seemed to make sense. But how were they connected? That's what Kenzie couldn't put together.

She took another bite, hoping the answers would come to her. Hoping that the answers were easy, and she just wasn't seeing them yet.

But she couldn't be sure how all of this fit together.

A moment later, her phone buzzed. She grabbed it from the table and glanced at the screen. She'd gotten a text message.

She clicked on it and a picture popped up.

She gasped at what she saw.

It was a photo of Jimmy James aboard *Seas the Day*.

Incriminating, undeniable evidence.

Someone had sent her a picture to taunt her. To threaten her.

Below that was a text message that read:

DON'T MISS **another opportunity or else.**

. . .

KENZIE'S BLOOD WENT COLD.

Somebody on this boat knew what was going on. They knew she'd missed the opportunity to set up the senator. They were keeping an eye on her.

The shiver raking through her only deepened.

This boat was no longer safe.

Now Kenzie had to figure out exactly what she was going to do about it.

AS JIMMY JAMES checked the boat, he kept his eyes open for Kenzie.

He knew her shift was almost over, so she was probably trying to finish up then get some shut-eye. He couldn't blame her.

He was still worried about her being here. About how the events of the past week were messing with her emotions. About how he'd blown things with her.

He paced the deck another moment, his thoughts churning.

The money he'd make from these charters would help him add to his nest egg. As soon as he had enough money, he was going to buy a bigger boat. He would start his own charter business.

He was going to make something of himself.

Jimmy James had promised to make his father proud. Though there was nothing wrong with being a workingman at the harbor, he didn't want to do this for the rest of his life. He wanted a better future for himself with more financial security. He wanted to do work that he found fulfilling.

Kenzie's image again filled his mind.

Would Kenzie see him differently if he made more of his life? She claimed she already thought a lot of him. Maybe she did. But he feared any of that would wear off over time.

Besides, he may have ruined things between them for good.

He let out a sigh and continued to monitor the boat.

CHAPTER THIRTY-SIX

KENZIE COLLECTED some leftover glasses and plates—her final task before she turned in for the evening.

But questions continued to swirl in her head.

Every time she thought about how someone on this boat could be responsible for Ashley's murder, a shudder went up her spine. How was she going to figure out what to do?

As she grabbed another plate, footsteps sounded behind her. She twirled around, halfway expecting to see someone threatening.

Instead, Sunni stepped toward her with a strange look on her face.

"Hey." Kenzie straightened, still holding the cleaning rag in her hands. "Do you need help with something?"

Sunni paused in front of Kenzie, that worried look intensifying. She lowered her voice as she said, "Actually, I need to tell you something."

Kenzie gripped her rag more tightly as she edged toward the chief stew. Based on the tone of Sunni's voice, whatever she had to say was serious.

"What's going on?" Kenzie asked quietly.

Sunni bit her bottom lip before glancing around as if to make sure nobody else was listening. Then she turned back to Kenzie, her features taut with apprehension. "Do you remember when I told you I saw that woman at the campground—the one you think was killed?"

"Ashley? Yes, of course. It's hard to forget that."

"Remember I told you I saw her arguing with another woman?"

"Yes." Tension edged up Kenzie's spine as she wondered where Sunni was going with this.

"I just realized who the woman was that I saw with Ashley."

Kenzie's lungs froze as she waited, desperate to hear the name on Sunni's lips.

AS JIMMY JAMES chatted with the senator's campaign manager, Alexandra, for a few minutes on the top deck, his phone rang. It was Axel.

He excused himself and stepped far enough away that no one could overhear.

If Axel was calling again, it must be important.

"You have news?" Jimmy James' shoulders felt tight with anticipation.

"Good evening to you also," Axel said, his tone dry. "As a matter of fact, I do."

"What's going on?"

"I looked into Thatcher's wife and what she was doing on the island. It turns out she flew into town yesterday morning to spend time with her husband."

Yesterday? "In other words, she can't be guilty . . ."

"She was caught on camera at a social gala out in Charlotte on the night of the murder. She's not who we're looking for."

"That's almost disappointing." Jimmy James frowned. She'd been a decent suspect.

"There's one other thing I discovered—almost by accident—or, as I prefer to call it . . . fortuitously."

Jimmy James glanced behind him and saw Alexandra had struck up a conversation with Owen and was totally distracted. "What's that?"

"Someone else was on the island the night of the murder—someone surprising. I happened to over-hear the owner of the Lantern Beach Sands Camp-ground talking about it while at The Crazy Chefette."

His heart thrummed in his ears. "Please, don't keep me in suspense."

"It was the one and only . . ."

CHAPTER THIRTY-SEVEN

KENZIE SHOOK her head and stepped closer to Sunni. Her gaze never left the chief stew's, however. She needed to know if she had heard correctly, if she'd understood the name Sunni had muttered.

Certainly, she hadn't.

"Are you positive that's who you saw?" Kenzie stared Sunni in the eye, desperate to see the truth.

Sunni nodded quickly, her tone almost somber. "I'm sure. The woman I saw arguing with Ashley was . . . Lori Williams. I just didn't realize who she was until now."

Kenzie's mind raced. "What took you so long to realize it was her?"

Sunni shrugged. "I didn't trust myself, I guess. I mean, she is the wife of a powerful political figure. But then I heard her say something during dinner—

that something should be a *piece of cake*. The way she said it . . . that's when I knew for sure that it was her. She said the exact same thing that night at the campground."

Kenzie ran a hand through her hair, trying to get her thoughts in place. What sense did that make? Lori Williams had been on the island earlier. Had she, for some reason, sought out Ashley Nelson and argued with her at a campground?

None of the pieces fit.

Kenzie sucked in a breath.

Unless they did.

Maybe Kenzie simply didn't want to face the truth—but as it pummeled her, she had no choice.

What if Lori Williams was the one behind Ashley's murder? Sure, Kenzie had seen a man on the boat with Ashley that night. But what if Lori had hired someone else to do her dirty work?

Lori seemed sweet. Unassuming. Not like the calculating type.

But sometimes turbulent undercurrents churned beneath still waters. Could that be the case with Lori?

If it was, what was Kenzie going to do about it? If the picture forming in her mind was accurate, more than one person on this boat could be in danger.

"What should we do?" Sunni's eyes were wide with fear. "Is this nothing? Am I overreacting?"

"We definitely need to tell Chief Chambers and Captain Gamble. Until we know exactly what's going on here, we should assume the worst."

Sunni glanced behind her again before rubbing her arms as if chilled. "I'm freaking out right now. I really don't like this."

"I know. I don't either. But you're *sure* that's who you saw?"

Sunni's gaze made it clear she didn't delight in sharing this news. "I'm positive. Lori Williams and Ashley were arguing about something. Then, that evening, Ashley was murdered."

Kenzie's mind continued to race. She remembered the person who'd threatened her in the car before the charter had departed. It had definitely been a man.

But it wasn't so much the person she was thinking about as much as it was the words he'd muttered.

Somebody wanted to set up Senator Williams to make him look like he wasn't the wholesome guy he presented himself to be.

Why would Lori Williams want to set up her husband like that?

As soon as the thought went through Kenzie's head, a footstep sounded behind her.

Kenzie glanced back to see who it was.

She sucked in a breath when she saw Lori

standing in the doorway with a gun in her hand and a crazy look in her eyes.

JIMMY JAMES NEEDED to find Kenzie. If his suspicions were correct, they could all be in danger right now.

He rushed from the bridge.

Where exactly was Kenzie? Her shift hadn't ended quite yet, so she should be somewhere in the interior. Did she have any idea the danger she was in?

It was Jimmy James' job to keep everybody on this boat safe.

But the situation they were in right now—anchored in the ocean—meant this whole boat was isolated.

With someone dangerous onboard.

This could end very poorly.

If the person behind these crimes was as calculated as Jimmy James thought, she'd twist this situation to make it appear none of this was her fault. He wasn't sure what that would look like. Murder-suicide? Someone accidentally falling overboard?

There were too many options for his comfort right now. But none of them ended well.

Jimmy James started toward the lower deck when he paused. Voices drifted through the window.

He sucked in a breath.

That was Kenzie.

And Lori Williams.

Based on what he was hearing, Kenzie was in trouble.

CHAPTER THIRTY-EIGHT

KENZIE DREW her gaze away from the gun in Lori's hand and locked her gaze with the woman's eyes instead.

"Lori, you don't want to do this," Kenzie muttered, even though she knew her words were useless.

Lori's nostrils flared as she stared at them. "You're right. I *don't* want to do this. But I heard everything you just said. I was standing around the corner. Clearly, you both know too much. I can't let you tell anyone what you learned."

Kenzie glanced around, looking for a way out.

But Lori stepped closer, blocking any potential escape routes. "Get into the game room behind you. Now."

Kenzie's throat tightened.

She knew what Lori was thinking—that they couldn't be out here in public. It was too risky.

But Kenzie also knew better than to comply. "What are you going to do with us if we go in there?"

"I'll figure that out when we get there," Lori said through gritted teeth. "For now, just move. We don't have much time."

In other words, they didn't have much time until someone found them and Lori's plan was ruined.

Would Lori dare shoot her and Sunni out here where someone might see her?

If the senator's wife was behind Ashley's murder, she'd be careful to cover her tracks here as well. She'd want to make this look like she wasn't involved in the crime, and being out here in public would put her at risk.

Maybe Kenzie could stall. Buy time.

"Why are you doing this?" Kenzie pushed Sunni behind her, sensing the woman's fear. Hearing her shallow breaths and gasps.

She was terrified—as anyone would be. Kenzie wasn't sure where she'd found her rush of courage. Perhaps it was pure survival instinct.

"Don't try to be a hero," Lori sneered. "Just do what I tell you or I'll shoot."

Sunni gasped before letting out a whimpering cry. "No . . ."

"You're not going to shoot us out here," Kenzie said. "That wouldn't fit your image. You know, the one that you were talking to me about earlier? You really have mastered the art of putting on facades, haven't you?"

Lori's eyes narrowed, her face transforming from warm and sweet to cold and prickly. "You wouldn't understand."

"But I do understand. My dad is a world-renowned brain surgeon. My whole life I've had to act a certain way. Do certain things. Follow certain paths."

"I feel like I'm following someone else's script, and I'm tired of it. No more." Lori waved the gun at them.

Kenzie needed to keep her talking. It would buy time. Maybe someone would find them. Help them.

Something.

"I just don't understand," Kenzie continued. "You have a good life. Why kill Ashley? Why threaten us right now?"

"I never wanted it to escalate like this." Lori shook her head a little too quickly to look like she was in her right mind. "But now I have to cover all my tracks. It's not what I wanted. None of this."

The gun trembled in her hands as the barrel still pointed at Kenzie's chest.

"Please don't do this!" Sunni cried.

Kenzie pushed the chief stew behind her again, afraid her outbursts would only intensify the situation.

"It's not too late to make things right," Kenzie murmured to Lori.

"Yes, it is! I have to cover up everything I've done. I won't go to jail for this. I'm already living in one kind of prison, and I don't want to move to another one."

Kenzie's gaze went to the gun again. She didn't think Lori would pull the trigger out here. But she was still dangerous.

The way the woman was trembling, she could flinch and . . . her finger could jerk. The gun could fire.

She swallowed hard.

Kenzie wasn't sure how she was going to stop this woman.

But she needed to think of something—and quickly.

JIMMY JAMES DIDN'T DARE LET Lori know he was so close. He remained hidden on the other side of the window, out of sight.

But alarm raced through him when he saw Eddie walking his way.

Jimmy James stepped back, blocking the first mate from going any farther. If Lori saw someone coming, she might get desperate and do something irreversible . . . and devastating.

"Everything okay, Captain?" A knot formed between Eddie's eyes as he stared at him.

"Listen, I need you to go to the bridge and call the Coast Guard. Tell them we have a situation, and we need backup."

Eddie's eyes widened. "What's going on?"

"Someone has pulled a gun on Kenzie and Sunni—"

Eddie's eyes widened and he looked like he wanted to lunge forward, to help. Jimmy James put a hand on his chest to stop him.

"Don't," Jimmy James muttered, putting a finger over his lips. "I've got this. You go do what I said."

Eddie started at him another moment before nodding and scurrying away.

Jimmy James waited until his first mate was out of sight before turning back to the scene inside. He leaned closer, trying to hear what was being said so he could plan his next move.

"I don't understand why you're doing this," Kenzie said.

"You have no idea how much my husband's career has cost me," Lori said. "You don't know what it's like."

"You tried to set up your husband and make it look like he was having an affair with Ashley Nelson, didn't you?" Shock coursed through Kenzie's voice.

"She agreed to it. She hated his stance against the Kinnakeet Society, and I paid well. It was going to be a win-win. All Ashley had to do was give me some incriminating evidence. I needed something that would get him kicked out of office."

Wow . . . this woman was truly desperate.

And out of her mind.

Jimmy James braced himself for the worst and remained on guard. Everything in him wanted to step into the scene. To barge in and demand Lori put down the gun.

But he'd been in enough difficult situations to know that wouldn't be a wise move right now. It would only set Lori off.

"But Ashley must have changed her mind," Kenzie said. "That's when you got desperate."

"She knew too much at that point. It could have been dangerous—to me as well as my husband. At least, if it looked like he had an affair then I'd get the sympathy. But if people know I'm the one who set him up? Then I might as well go into hiding for the rest of my life. That's not what I want. I want my freedom back."

"When Ashley backed out of your deal, you

hired someone to finish her off. If my guess is right, it was one of Thatcher Davenport's men."

Kenzie had done a great job putting this together. But with every new detail, a better picture of Lori Williams' derangement formed in his mind. This woman was desperate—and dangerous.

That didn't comfort him.

"I ran into them at an event and knew they'd be perfect," Lori said.

"Why did you even want to come here to Lantern Beach for a charter if you knew that could tie you to the murder?"

That was an excellent question. They seemed to keep coming from Kenzie.

If she decided not to be a yachtie, maybe she could look into police work.

Lori let out a sigh. "I'm the one who arranged this cruise, and I also arranged Ashley to join us and serve as a campaign strategist. She wasn't really a strategist. I knew that, but my husband didn't. He didn't even know her name. But I had a résumé worked up for Ashley to make it believable. We had our whole story worked out."

"And then?" Kenzie asked.

"I was paying her to hit on my husband. But she wanted to back out at the last minute. That wasn't part of our deal. By then, she knew too much. So I asked her to meet on *Seas the Day*. She didn't know what boat we were supposed to be on, so she didn't think anything of it. One of my guys finished her off there. Strangled her. There's less evidence to be left behind that way. No blood or anything incriminating."

"Before you hired those guys to kill Ashley, you came to Lantern Beach yourself and tried to convince Ashley to go along with the plan, didn't you?" Kenzie asked. "She was staying at the campground when you found her."

"How did you know that?" Lori's voice rang with accusation.

"Because I saw you!" Sunni shouted. "You're just evil!"

Lori let out a bitter laugh. "You know what? It doesn't matter. But, yes, I did. I told my husband I was going to a social event my old college roommate was hosting in Hatteras. I just happened to get there a little earlier and took a detour. But nobody was supposed to see me."

Silence stretched for a moment before Kenzie, her voice trembling, said, "You don't have to do this. There has to be another way. Can't you just talk to your husband? Use some good old-fashioned communication skills."

"You don't think I've tried to do that?" Lori snapped. "All Luke cares about is politics. That's the way it's been for a long time, and nothing's going to change. You should have just done what I told you to do, and we wouldn't be in this situation right now."

Jimmy James' breath caught. *What she told Kenzie to do?* What did that even mean?

"I couldn't do it," Kenzie said. "I can't set somebody up and ruin them. That's not in my nature."

Jimmy James sucked in a breath. Lori had told Kenzie to set up the senator? Had Kenzie even entertained that idea? Why hadn't she told him about her dilemma?

"As soon as I finish you two off, I'm going to send those pictures of Captain Gamble aboard *Seas the Day* to the authorities. You should have just listened. It would have solved all our problems."

Dread pooled in Jimmy James' stomach. *That* was the leverage that Lori had held over Kenzie.

Someone must have seen him looking for Kenzie onboard that yacht and taken photos. He only wished she'd come to him with this problem instead of carrying that burden alone.

"Now, enough talking!" Lori barked. "I need to get this over with. You two, get into that game room. Now."

Jimmy James had to act. He knew as soon as they were out of sight, Lori would pull the trigger. Then she'd figure out a way to cover up her crime.

She seemed to be the master at letting other people take the fall for what she did.

But not anymore.

As he heard another footstep behind him, he froze.

What now?

CHAPTER THIRTY-NINE

"WE'RE NOT GOING in that game room." Kenzie knew she and Sunni would be goners if they did.

Lori's eyes widened, and her nostrils flared when she heard Kenzie's defiance. She waved the gun, the crazy gleam in her gaze growing stronger by the moment. "What do you mean you're not going in that room? I'm the one with the gun. Do I need to remind you of that?"

"But you're not going to shoot us out here," Kenzie said. "There will be no way to cover up your crimes if you do."

Lori's eyes narrowed as if she didn't appreciate Kenzie's observation. "I'll figure out a way to make this work. Believe me. I will. What you don't know is that I'm one of my husband's top political strategists.

It's what I do, albeit my work is all behind the scenes and I get no credit."

The bitterness in Lori's words helped Kenzie form a better picture of what was going on here. Someone with this much natural talent in manipulation should be in politics. So much of what happened was about spin, and Lori appeared to be a master of twisting the truth.

"How will you make it look as if it's our fault if you shoot us out here in the open?" Kenzie asked.

Lori's eyes narrowed, but she still appeared undeterred. "Maybe I'll tie it in with the captain's crime-filled past. I'll claim you're his little minions, and you caught me asking too many questions. I don't know exactly what it'll be, but I'll figure out something. You shouldn't doubt me."

"You're going to go to jail if you shoot us," Kenzie reminded her.

"You don't know what you're talking about." Lori's words flew from her lips, faster and higher pitched by the moment.

Kenzie was getting to her. Good. That's what she needed to do—to throw Lori off balance.

Because Kenzie wasn't bluffing. She didn't think Lori would shoot her and Sunni out in the open. Even if she did, any of those excuses Lori had come up with wouldn't hold up in court.

Besides, if the three of them stayed here for

much longer, somebody was bound to walk past at some point. Somebody who could help them. Who could stop Lori.

Preferably Jimmy James.

Kenzie's heart squeezed at the thought of him.

She hadn't realized how much she had come to depend on the man in the short time they'd known each other. But she had. He always had her back.

Kenzie didn't take that for granted, even with everything that had transpired between the two of them.

At once, Lori lunged forward and grabbed Sunni's arm. She jerked the chief stew toward her and shoved the gun against her temple.

Sunni gasped, her eyes filled with fear.

"Do what I say, or I'll shoot your friend." Lori's voice cracked. "Don't even think I won't do it."

Kenzie's breath caught when she saw the terror on Sunni's face.

It was one thing to put her own life on the line. But it was an entirely different story to put someone else's life in danger.

Kenzie's thoughts raced as she tried to figure out exactly what she would do.

Just then, voices sounded in the distance.

This was it, Kenzie realized. This was her chance to make a move. Maybe her only chance.

But if things went wrong . . .

She couldn't let herself think about it.

As Lori quickly glanced toward the sound, Kenzie tackled her. Their bodies collided onto the teak floor, and Kenzie wrestled her, trying to get the gun. But Lori swung it around wildly, keeping it just out of reach.

"Run!" Kenzie told Sunni. "Get help!"

Sunni stared at her for a moment before darting past them toward a door on the other side of the room.

As she disappeared, Kenzie slammed Lori's arm onto the floor.

The gun slipped from her grasp and slid across the wooden floor.

Kenzie stared at it, stretching to reach it. But the weapon was too far away.

She'd have to let go of Lori in order to grab it.

"Lori? What's going on here?"

Kenzie's stomach clenched. She didn't have to look up to know who the voice belonged to.

Senator Williams.

Even worse, Kenzie knew exactly how this looked.

She was on top of Lori as if she'd been the aggressor in this situation.

Lori's face had instantly transformed into a victim-like expression as she glanced back at her husband.

Kenzie jumped to her feet and grabbed the gun, her survival more important than her reputation right now. Only once she gripped it in her hands did she say, "Your wife tried to shoot me and Sunni."

Williams' bodyguards appeared and rushed toward Kenzie, ready to snatch the gun away. But she pointed the barrel at them, warning them to stay back.

Kenzie braced herself for whatever was going to happen next.

The senator rushed toward his wife, helping her to her feet as the two of them scowled at her.

Based on the look on the senator's face, he didn't believe a word that Kenzie said. His wrong assumptions could get her hurt—or even worse.

Just as the thought filled her mind, one of his security guards grabbed her arms. The other snatched the gun from her.

Kenzie released a breath.

Suddenly, she no longer had the upper hand.

EVERYTHING HAPPENED FAST.

Too fast.

Just as things escalated inside, Eddie had rushed back toward Jimmy James, ready to run into the salon himself. Jimmy James stopped him, not wanting to make the situation more tense.

Instead, he peered through the window.

Two bodyguards had Kenzie by the arms. They'd taken the gun as they restrained her.

Lori cried in her husband's arms and scooted back as if she feared for her life.

Senator Williams and his men must have come in from the other door across the room.

Jimmy James had to get in there.

Now.

He stepped through one of the doors leading into the salon and paused, muscles bristling with tension as he tried to keep a cool head. "What's going on here? Why are you holding a gun to my steward?"

"Lori tried to kill me," Kenzie rushed.

Senator Williams gawked, looking appalled at the mere suggestion. "That's not true. Your steward tried to kill my wife."

"We all know that's not what happened, don't we?" Jimmy James looked at Lori, his gaze pointed and unwavering.

"Luke . . ." Lori looked up at her husband, desperation cracking her voice. "All these people want Sampson to win. This has all been a setup. All of it. I'm so sorry. I should have looked deeper into their backgrounds. I . . . I failed you."

The senator's gaze went back to Jimmy James and then Kenzie. "Is that true? Are you all working for Sampson? Has the political game gotten this twisted and evil that he'd take it this far?"

"Don't listen to anything she says." Kenzie tugged against the grip of the security guard, her gaze feisty and undeterred as she stared at the senator. "Your wife has been lying to you this whole time. She tried to set you up and make it look like you were having an affair. All so you'd leave the political world."

Senator Williams looked back at Lori and shook his head. "Lori would never do something like that. She loves our life. Why are you trying to make her look bad? Are you that desperate?"

The severity of the situation hit Jimmy James. He knew how hard it would be for the senator to believe the truth. But with Sunni, Jimmy James, and Kenzie as witnesses, how could Williams ultimately deny it?

Then again, Jimmy James had seen some crazy things in his life. People believed what they wanted to believe. They believed what fit their narrative. And they twisted the facts in their minds to make that happen.

For that reason, he knew the situation could get uglier before it got better.

"Let Kenzie go." Jimmy James turned to the security guards and placed his hands on his hips. "Take your hands off her."

"Don't listen to him," Williams rushed. "Don't let her go. She's dangerous."

Jimmy James puffed his chest out. "I'm in charge on this boat."

"Do you know who I am?" The senator thumped his own chest, his eyes so wide he almost looked delusional. "I have enough power to make your life miserable. Believe me, I do."

"I'm the captain of this boat. I have authority over you and your bodyguards. And I'm telling you that you need to let Kenzie go. Don't make me take matters into my own hands." His voice came out a low growl as his jaw muscles flexed.

Williams sent a look to his bodyguards. The next instant, both aimed their weapons—one gun pointed at Kenzie and the other at Jimmy James.

Jimmy James sucked in a breath.

These people honestly thought Jimmy James and his crew were the bad guys here. Lori's manipulation had worked. She'd twisted the truth enough that no one knew exactly what to believe.

Somehow, he had to make everyone see what was really going on.

Before he could say anything, Lori let out a grueling sob and clung to her husband. "I thought I was going to die, honey. Thank you so much for saving me. You have no idea how frightened I was."

This woman was a great actress. It seemed as if her husband had fallen hook, line, and sinker for what she was selling.

Jimmy James looked at Kenzie, and the two of them exchanged a glance.

This might just be harder than either of them had anticipated.

CHAPTER FORTY

KENZIE COULDN'T LET Lori win. Even though she knew the truth would come out in the long run, that might not stop another tragedy from happening in the more immediate future.

Considering the fact that one bodyguard had a gun pointed at her and the other guard had a gun pointed at Jimmy James, this wasn't looking good.

"She's playing you." Kenzie stared at Senator Williams, desperate to make him see the truth. "Lori wants you out of office, and she was willing to go to extremes to make that happen. She even went as far as to commit murder."

"I don't believe you!" The senator shook his head, his chest rising and falling too rapidly as he kept an arm around his wife. "You need to stop talking."

"You shouldn't trust them." Lori sobbed again before sending an accusing look at Kenzie and Jimmy James. "They're trying to make me look bad. Trying to cover up their own political agenda. Don't let them win. Please."

"She's the one trying to win." Kenzie tried to jerk her arm out of the bodyguard's grip again, but he held too tightly. "Your wife orchestrated all this. She even killed that woman. Ashley Nelson—your new political strategist."

The senator's mouth fell open, and he glanced at his wife as if a moment of doubt filled his mind.

Then he looked back at Kenzie. "You're wrong. Lori didn't even know that woman. Neither of us did. You're just trying to make me doubt my wife. Trying to turn me against her."

"Your wife is a dangerous woman," Kenzie said.

"Stop talking!" Senator Williams sliced his hand through the air. "I need to figure out what's going on here."

"The Coast Guard is on their way," Eddie announced.

"Great," Senator Williams said. "We'll just wait until they get here and then they'll sort everything out. In the meantime, no one better make any moves."

But it was too late. The rest of the crew had gathered around to watch this scene play out. Thankfully, the senator's kids were already in bed and didn't have to witness this.

"What she's saying is true." Sunni seemed to break out of her trance-like state as she stepped back into the room. "Your wife pulled the gun on us, Senator Williams. She wanted to make it look like she was defending herself or that Kenzie and I had turned on each other. Anything to make it seem that Kenzie and I were the aggressors. But that's not true."

"Stop talking!" The senator's voice rose, and his eyes grew even wider. "Stop trying to make Lori look bad. I won't stand for it. Do you understand?"

Jimmy James inched closer but kept his voice even as not to provoke anymore outbursts. "Think about your wife. She grew up poor in a small West Virginia town. But you transformed her into the political powerhouse she is today. You know just as well as anyone else that when she's not in the public eye, she's a different person. She's mastered putting on masks. You can't deny that fact. You helped make her that way."

Kenzie glanced up at Jimmy James as if confused as to where he had gotten that information.

"You don't know what you're talking about." Disbelief stained the senator's voice.

"You know we're speaking the truth." Jimmy James continued to creep closer, taking steps so small they were almost indiscernible. "You're just in denial. There's no way that you're going to walk away from this unscathed."

"He's lying!" Lori nearly hissed. "When people hear about what happened to us on this charter, your numbers are going to soar, honey. You're going to get the sympathy vote."

"I want people to vote for me because they believe in what I stand for." Something in his voice changed as he said the words.

Was he realizing the truth?

"In an election like the one we're in, you don't want to turn down any votes. Isn't that what you always say?" More bitterness edged Lori's voice.

The senator glanced at his wife and his expression tensed. Had he seen Lori in a different light? Did he have a realization about what was actually going on here?

Jimmy James prayed that was the case.

It might be the only way that they were going to get out of this situation unharmed.

KENZIE WISHED SHE WAS STRONGER. But it didn't matter how many spinning classes she'd taken, she knew she wouldn't be able to take down the bodyguard holding tightly to her arm.

He was much larger than she was. Plus, he had a gun.

As she felt the pressure building in the room, she knew this could turn out poorly.

Their best chance of surviving was if they could convince Senator Williams that his wife was a fraud.

"You wouldn't do this, would you?" Senator Williams glanced at his wife, a touch of disbelief in his voice.

"They're all lying to you." Lori wiped faked tears from beneath her eyes. "Don't believe them. That's what they want."

"Did you really go to that event at your college roommate's house?"

"Of course. You don't believe me?" Her voice trembled as if she were afraid.

"I didn't see you in any of the pictures. I looked."

"Well, you didn't look hard enough." Her voice hardened. "You know I'd never kill anyone. That's preposterous. Don't let them get to you."

"The truth is, I had a lot of questions about this strategist you set up for me." Senator Williams' voice sounded more aloof, more cautious. "I tried to look into her and even asked a few colleagues about her. No one had heard of her."

Kenzie's heart thudded harder into her chest. Maybe they'd be able to convince the senator that his wife was guilty after all.

"What are you saying, Luke?" Tears glimmered in Lori's eyes.

"I'm saying that things are starting to make a little bit more sense." The senator stepped away from her.

Kenzie exchanged another glance with Jimmy James.

Maybe this was it. Maybe this was the moment where everyone would come to their senses. Lori could be subdued. The Coast Guard would arrive and arrest the senator's wife. And this would all be over.

Was it hoping too much to believe that was true?

CHAPTER FORTY-ONE

JIMMY JAMES PRAYED the senator would see the whole truth for what it was. But he knew that the process—the reckoning—would be difficult.

The senator seemed to truly love his wife.

What Jimmy James wasn't sure about was where the senator would go with this conversation.

"You set this all up, didn't you?" Williams asked.

Lori gasped, her expression morphing into outraged offense. "What are you talking about? You believe *them*? You're letting them get to you?"

"What Kenzie said is true, isn't it?" His voice hardened. "You wanted to make it look like I had an affair so I'd get out of politics. You begged and pleaded with me, and that never did any good. So, you took matters into your own hands."

The despair on Lori's face disappeared as if

someone had flipped a switch. Instead, her expression hardened. "You never did listen to me, Luke."

"That's not true. You're great at helping me plan my next political move." Senator Williams shook his head, his eyes beginning to harden. "But you always have liked getting your way."

"Who doesn't? That doesn't mean I would kill."

Senator Williams stared at her, his gaze colder than before. "The truth is that I saw you talking to one of Thatcher Davenport's bodyguards at an event last week. I just didn't put together what you were doing. But now it all makes sense."

The next instant, the senator strode across the room and snatched a gun from his bodyguard.

He pointed it at his wife.

Jimmy James felt his heartbeat ratchet up.

This wasn't the way this was supposed to play out.

Nobody was going to get killed on Jimmy James' watch.

Not if he had anything to do about it.

KENZIE FELT the bodyguard beside her shift as if he didn't know what to do either.

This whole situation spun out of control, and the air was filled with frenzied emotions and panic.

Now they needed to figure out exactly what to do about it.

As the senator held the gun on his wife, Lori rose to full height, something almost evil filling her already dark eyes.

"I've made you who you are today," she growled as she nearly crouched toward him. "That doesn't mean I don't regret it. You're a senator because of me."

His eyes seemed to burn into Lori's. "All you've done is nag me. Now we finally have what we've always wanted, and you no longer like the position that we're in. It's nearly impossible to make you happy."

"Sometimes you get what you want, and you realize that you should have never wanted it in the first place."

"I can't believe you did this to me . . ." The senator raised the gun higher.

Lori's face went pale as if she realized he actually might pull the trigger. "Luke . . . you don't want to do this. Please."

"I did this for you." He practically spat out the words. "I thought it was what you wanted."

"Luke . . ."

The senator was thinking about pulling the trigger, wasn't he?

Jimmy James seemed to sense that also.

He stepped forward, his motions steady and calm. "Maybe we can all just talk this through without any guns."

"You've already done enough." Senator Williams narrowed his eyes as he glanced at Jimmy James. "Now you need to stay out of it."

Kenzie felt her breath catch. How was this ordeal going to end? She wasn't sure.

Please, Lord. Help us!

"Guns never solve anything," Jimmy James said.

"Funny you say that, because you look like the kind of person who's been in a few fights in his day," the senator sneered. "The type who'd use a gun to solve a problem."

"Well, appearances can be deceiving. The two of you are a case in point." Truth rang through Jimmy James' words.

The senator's eyes narrowed, and he abruptly turned the gun from his wife to Jimmy James. "Don't talk to me like that. I'm doing my best. Can't anyone understand that? I just can't make everyone happy, and I'm tired of trying."

"Senator—" the bodyguard started.

Williams' eyes nearly bulged from their sockets. "I'm tired of talking!"

His hands went to the trigger as his gaze focused on Jimmy James.

"No!" Kenzie shouted.

Before the senator could pull the trigger, she lunged toward him. The bodyguard tried to grab her, but Kenzie slipped out of his grasp.

Her hands hit the senator's shoulders, and he tumbled to the deck.

As he fell, the gun went off before slipping from his grasp.

She held her breath, uncertain where the bullet had gone.

Had it hit her? Was the pain not registering yet?

When she heard a cry across the room, she realized the truth.

Lori Williams had been hit instead.

Jimmy James grabbed Senator Williams' arms and jerked him from the floor. Then the captain shoved his arms behind him, subduing him.

Kenzie snatched the gun from the floor before the wrong person grabbed it instead.

A moment later, she heard the welcome sound of the Coast Guard announcing themselves as they flooded the boat.

Maybe this could all really be over.

She prayed that was the case.

CHAPTER FORTY-TWO

STARS SPARKLED OVERHEAD, an avid audience to the events that had unfolded. Jimmy James stood on the aft deck and ran a hand over his face as he tried to comprehend the surreal situation that had happened on his boat.

The Coast Guard had boarded. Arrests had been made. Evidence was being collected.

The crew was separated for questioning.

Kenzie was being treated by a medic. She'd gotten a scrape on her arm when she tackled Lori.

But it was all over now, and everyone was okay— except for Lori, but she *would* be okay. The wound had been mostly surface.

This yacht seemed to be a magnet for trouble.

And trouble was the exact thing Jimmy James was trying to stay away from.

As he sucked in a deep breath, his friend Axel strode up to him. When he'd alerted the Coast Guard, they'd let him come along for the rescue, thinking his expertise could come in handy.

"Hey, man," Axel murmured. "You sure you're okay?"

Jimmy James nodded and took another sip of water from his bottle. "I'm just glad the Coast Guard arrived when they did."

"Me too."

Despite the fact that Lori was still claiming to be a victim, they had numerous witnesses as to what had happened, and Jimmy James and his crew should all be in the clear. He'd already made a call to Mr. Robertson to let him know what had happened. As expected, Robertson hadn't been happy.

But Jimmy James knew that none of this was his fault.

He thought that being here on this charter was what he wanted.

On second thought, maybe it wasn't. Maybe working for the elite rich wasn't what he was called to do. Maybe managing a team of strong-willed yachties was more than he could handle. And maybe crime would always follow him, no matter how hard he tried to leave that life behind.

The senator and his people had been escorted from *Almost Paradise* onto a Coast Guard boat. Once back in Lantern Beach, the children's grandmother would meet them and somehow try to explain why their parents had been arrested.

Another coastguardsman would remain aboard *Almost Paradise* while they headed back to Lantern Beach to dock. More evidence would be taken, the crew would be questioned, and they'd go through the whole song and dance again.

Jimmy James was just happy this was nearly over.

His eyes searched the crowd again for Kenzie. The two of them hadn't had a moment to talk since this had all started.

He desperately wanted to know how she was doing. How she was *really* doing. Beyond the physical. She was clearly shaken, as was everybody who'd witnessed what had happened.

But Kenzie was much stronger than most people gave her credit for. What she'd done had been brave. It had required courage and selflessness.

Jimmy James was proud to call her a friend right now. She'd been willing to sacrifice her life for his. That wasn't something he'd ever been able to say about anyone before.

But there was no way he'd ever want someone like Kenzie to be hurt or killed in place of him.

No way.

As Axel began talking to a coastie, Jimmy James

stepped across the deck and found Kenzie sitting in a lounge chair.

He and Kenzie didn't have to say anything to each other. Instead, he pulled her up into his arms and gave her the biggest bear hug he could muster.

"I'm glad you're okay," he whispered in her ear.

"I'm glad you're okay." She pulled away and offered a glassy smile, almost appearing like she wanted to cry.

Tonight's events had really shaken her up, hadn't they?

She drew in a deep breath as if trying to pull herself together. Questions raced through her gaze. "Have you heard anything about Thatcher's bodyguards yet? The ones who strangled Ashley and disposed of her body?"

"Cassidy and her crew are on their way to arrest them. From what I understand, the work for an agency called the Dagger Group. Lori paid them both to do her dirty work. They had absolutely no loyalty to Thatcher—or to anyone. Their allegiance was only to money."

"What about their alibis? The one they supposedly had on the night of the murder?"

"Axel told me they slipped out of the restaurant and paid some people to vouch for them."

Kenzie let out a sigh. "How did they manage to

hide Ashley's body like they did? That still doesn't make sense to me."

"From what I heard, the two of them had a small rubber dinghy at the bottom of Thatcher's yacht. That's where Ashley fell. Then the two of them took her body out to deeper water and chained an anchor around her so she'd sink. The black boat combined with their dark clothing helped them to blend in with the darkness and water, which is why no one saw them."

"How did that guy get off the boat before the police were able to find him?"

"Most likely, when you came inside to get me, whichever bodyguard strangled Ashley jumped in the water, swam to the boat where his partner waited, and they pulled away before anyone found them. Easy peasy lemon squeezy."

"What about that lingerie I found?"

He shrugged. "Who knows what Thatcher had going on the side . . . ?"

Kenzie rubbed her arms as if she were chilled. Her gaze wandered as she stared in the distance, no doubt filled with bad memories of what had transpired this evening.

He wished he could take those images away from her—but he could only be there to support her instead. He prayed that was enough—and that she didn't push him away.

Her gaze fluttered back up to meet his. "Jimmy James . . . when we were in the standoff in the salon . . . I knew you'd do whatever you could to protect me. I just want to let you know how much that means to me."

"I'm glad you know that. Because it's true. I don't want anyone to ever hurt you. Including me." He shifted. "But you were the real hero back there. They threatened to set me up, didn't they? If you didn't do what they told you?"

She shrugged. "They wanted me to put myself in a compromising position with the senator. Lori was probably going to take pictures and blame them on the bodyguards. That's my guess."

"I'm sorry you were put in that position. You should have told me."

"I just keep thinking about those photos of you on *Seas the Day*. You've worked so hard, and you only boarded that boat to help me. What if you went to prison and—"

"You should have told me."

She frowned. "Maybe. I didn't know what to do."

"You can always talk to me, Kenzie."

She smiled softly. "Thank you. Maybe we make a pretty good team."

"Maybe we do."

She pressed her lips together as moisture filled her eyes. "Jimmy James . . ."

He shook his head. "How about you and I talk later? Once we get back to Lantern Beach. Can we do that?"

She stared at him another moment, more emotions welling in her eyes. "Yes, I would love that. I need to just go somewhere I can breathe. Where I can forget about all of this."

"I know just the place," Jimmy James said.

"You do?"

He nodded. "I'll show you."

"I'll look forward to it."

He just hoped that next time he would be able to express his emotions a little more clearly.

CHAPTER FORTY-THREE

"WHERE EXACTLY ARE YOU TAKING ME?" Kenzie glanced at the water surrounding Jimmy James' Bayliner.

She'd thought he was taking her to an actual destination, but the ocean seemed to be the end point instead.

"I'm taking you to the place I think has the best sunsets in the whole entire world," Jimmy James said as he idled forward. "I want to share it with you."

"So, you're not ditching me in the middle of the inlet where no one will ever find me?"

He grinned. "I think you've been reading too many crime novels."

"Reading too many? You mean, *living* too many."

He chuckled as he continued to slowly direct the

boat forward. "You're right. I can't argue that. Plus, you know I'd never hurt you."

"You're right. I do know that." She cast him a soft smile as she gripped the edge of the cockpit, trying to hold steady as rolling waves rocked the watercraft.

In fact, she knew beyond a doubt that this man would protect her with his life.

A few seconds later, he cut the motor—still in the middle of the water. He dropped the anchor before turning toward her. "We're here."

"Here?" She still had no idea what was happening here.

"You'll see," he muttered.

As Jimmy James hopped off the boat, she expected him to sink in the water. Instead, he stood beside the boat and held up his hands to help her out.

Kenzie realized that the water was surprisingly shallow in this area.

A sandbar, she realized. They were all around these barrier islands, which made them tricky to navigate, from what she'd heard.

She tested the water's depth, just to make sure she was correct, before sliding out of the boat and walking away from the edge, onto firmer sand.

"If I said I'd always believed you could walk on water, no one could argue." Jimmy James winked at her as he reached back into his boat.

"You're full of one-liners this evening."

"What can I say?"

She turned toward the western horizon, and her breath caught. The sun sank over the water, the clouds creating an awe-inspiring smear of colors and shapes. This was what he'd brought her to see, wasn't it?

"It's beautiful," she murmured, already mesmerized at the sight of it.

Jimmy James grabbed a beach chair from the back of the boat and set it on the sandbar. Kenzie settled on the bright orange fabric, anxious to continue watching the greatest show of all—the sun disappearing beneath the horizon.

Jimmy James placed a cooler and a matching chair beside her and sat with her. He pulled some bottled lemonade from the cooler and grabbed a paper bag filled with homemade cupcakes from a bakery in town.

Kenzie accepted a lemon-flavored treat and let the delicious flavors wash over her tongue. Lemonade, lemon cupcakes, and a sunset? The moment couldn't be more perfect.

"Sometimes you can see dolphins out here." Jimmy James pointed to the water in the distance as if visualizing it. "I like to come here when I need to think. Not many people know this sandbar is here."

"Do you bring a lot of people here?" She raised her eyebrows in curiosity.

He grabbed her hand and squeezed it. "You're the only one."

Surprise—and a touch of delight—raced through her. Kenzie had to admit that she liked knowing she was special to Jimmy James. The realization made her feel like she was floating on the clouds.

Jimmy James leaned toward her, his gaze searching hers. "Kenzie, do you know what a dead reckoning is?"

She shrugged, curious where he was going with this. "I've heard the term before. But I can't say I know for sure."

"It's a term used in boating when you're trying to navigate unfamiliar waters without any radar or other equipment you might normally use to make the passage."

"Interesting." She still wasn't sure what he was getting at.

"From the moment I met you, Kenzie, I felt like I've been navigating unfamiliar but exciting waters. I feel like I'm heading toward a destination I've always dreamed about going to but never thought I'd actually be able to reach."

"I'm the destination?" Her throat tightened.

"Maybe analogies aren't my thing." He flashed a

smile. "But I guess I'm just trying to say that part of me doesn't feel like I know what I'm doing. I want so badly to do the right thing by you. I want to be the person you deserve. I'm just not sure I know how to do that."

Kenzie pressed her lips together, sensing he wasn't finished yet. She gave him time to compose his thoughts.

"I know I messed things up with you after your dad came to town," he continued. "I just want to say that I'm sorry. You're one of the best things to ever happen to me. I don't want to ruin that. But I know I did, and I deeply regret that."

Kenzie licked her lips, praying she had the right words and that she could speak from her heart. "I know you have a good heart. I do. I can even see where you might have thought breaking up with me was the right thing. But that doesn't take away any of the hurt your decision caused."

"How could I make it better?" He squeezed her hand, his gaze latched onto hers.

A rush of warmth flooded her. Kenzie definitely still had feelings for Jimmy James, despite the hurt.

She looked away and stared across the water as the sun continued to sink lower.

After everything that happened, she might think that being alone in such an isolated place with Jimmy James would be unnerving. But it wasn't. She knew she could trust him. Knew he'd always look out for her.

That was a realization she'd always treasure.

But still . . . there were other issues she needed to deal with, and it was better to tackle them head-on than to ignore them or pretend as if they didn't exist.

"I don't know that I'm ready to jump back into a relationship yet." Kenzie's throat ached as she spoke. "It actually takes a lot for me to open up my heart."

Some of the hope faded from Jimmy James' eyes.

"But I might be willing to one day," Kenzie rushed.

His eyes brightened again, but the intensity remained. "What needs to change for you to possibly consider that?"

"I guess I just need to see with my own eyes that I'm not going to be hurt again."

"See with your own eyes?" He tilted his head as if confused.

"I don't want to put myself in a position where I try to take a plunge only to have the person jumping with me back out at the last minute."

"Kenzie—"

"I know." She held up her hand to stop him. "I understand what you told me, and maybe part of me even appreciates where you're coming from. I guess I just need time to test the waters and make sure that the ground beneath me is as stable as I want it to be.

Maybe exploring these waters with you is a bit of a dead reckoning for me too."

He pressed his lips together and brushed a hand across her cheek. "I will do whatever I need to do to prove that I won't make the same mistakes over again."

Kenzie felt her emotions catch in her throat. "I hope that's true. I hope that the two of us . . . I hope we can figure things out. I guess I'm just saying I need a little time."

"I'll give you all the time that you need."

She smiled at his words before scooting her chair closer to his. She rested her head on Jimmy James' shoulder as she glanced out at the last glimpse of the sun disappearing on the horizon.

The nice part about sunsets was looking forward to the sunrise the next morning.

And that was exactly what Kenzie was doing now.

~~~

If you enjoyed this book, please consider leaving a review!

COMING NEXT: TIPPING POINT

Get Your Copy Here!

ALSO BY CHRISTY BARRITT:

LANTERN BEACH MYSTERIES

Hidden Currents

You can take the detective out of the investigation, but you can't take the investigator out of the detective. A notorious gang puts a bounty on Detective Cady Matthews's head after she takes down their leader, leaving her no choice but to hide until she can testify at trial. But her temporary home across the country on a remote North Carolina island isn't as peaceful as she initially thinks. Living under the new identity of Cassidy Livingston, she struggles to keep her investigative skills tucked away, especially after a body washes ashore. When local police bungle the murder investigation, she can't resist stepping in. But Cassidy is supposed to be keeping a low profile. One wrong move could lead to both her discovery and her demise. Can she bring justice to the island . . . or will the hidden currents surrounding her pull her under for good?

Flood Watch

The tide is high, and so is the danger on Lantern Beach. Still in hiding after infiltrating a dangerous gang, Cassidy Livingston just has to make it a few more months before she can testify at trial and resume her old life. But trouble keeps finding her, and Cassidy is pulled into a local investigation after a man mysteriously disappears from the island she now calls home. A recurring nightmare from her time undercover only muddies things, as does a visit from the parents of her handsome ex-Navy SEAL neighbor. When a friend's life is threatened, Cassidy must make choices that put her on the verge of blowing her cover. With a flood watch on her emotions and her life in a tangle, will Cassidy find the truth? Or will her past finally drown her?

Storm Surge

A storm is brewing hundreds of miles away, but its effects are devastating even from afar. Laid-back, loose, and light: that's Cassidy Livingston's new motto. But when a makeshift boat with a bloody cloth inside washes ashore near her oceanfront home, her detective instincts shift into gear . . . again. Seeking clues isn't the only thing on her mind—romance is heating up with next-door neighbor and former Navy SEAL Ty Chambers as well. Her heart wants the love and stability she's longed for her entire life. But her hidden identity only leads to a tidal wave of turbulence. As more answers emerge about the boat, the danger around her rises, creating a treacherous swell that threatens to reveal her past. Can Cassidy mind her own business, or will the storm surge of violence and corruption that has washed ashore on Lantern Beach leave her life in wreckage?

Dangerous Waters

Danger lurks on the horizon, leaving only two choices: find shelter or flee. Cassidy Livingston's new identity has begun to feel as comfortable as her favorite sweater. She's been tucked away on Lantern Beach for weeks, waiting to testify against a deadly gang, and is settling in to a new life she wants to last forever. When she thinks she spots someone malevolent from her past, panic swells inside her. If an enemy has found her, Cassidy won't be the only one who's a target. Everyone she's come to love will also be at risk. Dangerous waters threaten to pull her into an overpowering chasm she may never escape. Can Cassidy survive what lies ahead? Or has the tide fatally turned against her?

Perilous Riptide

Just when the current seems safer, an unseen danger emerges and threatens to destroy everything. When Cassidy Livingston finds a journal hidden deep in the recesses of her ice cream truck, her curiosity kicks into high gear. Islanders suspect that Elsa, the journal's owner, didn't die accidentally. Her final entry indicates their suspicions might be correct and that what Elsa observed on her final night may have led to her demise. Against the advice of Ty Chambers, her former Navy SEAL boyfriend, Cassidy taps into her detective skills and hunts for answers. But her search only leads to a skeletal body and trouble for both of them. As helplessness threatens to drown her, Cassidy is desperate to turn back time. Can Cassidy find what she needs to navigate the perilous situation? Or will the riptide surrounding her threaten everyone and everything Cassidy loves?

Deadly Undertow

The current's fatal pull is powerful, but so is one detective's will to live. When someone from Cassidy Livingston's past shows up on Lantern Beach and warns her of impending peril, opposing currents collide, threatening to drag her under. Running would be easy. But leaving would break her heart. Cassidy must decipher between the truth and lies, between reality and deception. Even more importantly, she must decide whom to trust and whom to fear. Her life depends on it. As danger rises and answers surface, everything Cassidy thought she knew is tested. In order to survive, Cassidy must take drastic measures and end the battle against the ruthless gang DH-7 once and for all. But if her final mission fails, the consequences will be as deadly as the raging undertow.

LANTERN BEACH ROMANTIC SUSPENSE

Tides of Deception

Change has come to Lantern Beach: a new police chief, a new season, and . . . a new romance? Austin Brooks has loved Skye Lavinia from the moment they met, but the walls she keeps around her seem impenetrable. Skye knows Austin is the best thing to ever happen to her. Yet she also knows that if he learns the truth about her past, he'd be a fool not to run. A chance encounter brings secrets bubbling to the surface, and danger soon follows. Are the life-threatening events plaguing them really accidents . . . or is someone trying to send a deadly message? With the tides on Lantern Beach come deception and lies. One question remains—who will be swept away as the water shifts? And will it bring the end for Austin and Skye, or merely the beginning?

Shadow of Intrigue

For her entire life, Lisa Garth has felt like a supporting character in the drama of life. The designation never bothered her—until now. Lantern Beach, where she's settled and runs a popular restaurant, has boarded up for the season. The slower pace leaves her with too much time alone. Braden Dillinger came to Lantern Beach to try to heal. The former Special Forces officer returned from battle with invisible scars and diminished hope. But his recovery is hampered by the fact that an unknown enemy is trying to kill him. From the moment Lisa and Braden meet, danger ignites around them, and both are drawn into a web of intrigue that turns their lives upside down. As shadows creep in, will Lisa and Braden be able to shine a light on the peril around them? Or will the encroaching darkness turn their worst nightmares into reality?

Storm of Doubt

A pastor who's lost faith in God. A romance writer who's lost faith in love. A faceless man with a deadly obsession. Nothing has felt right in Pastor Jack Wilson's world since his wife died two years ago. He hoped coming to Lantern Beach might help soothe the ragged edges of his soul. Instead, he feels more alone than ever. Novelist Juliette Grace came to the island to hide away. Though her professional life has never been better, her personal life has imploded. Her husband left her and a stalker's threats have grown more and more dangerous. When Jack saves Juliette from an attack, he sees the terror in her gaze and knows he must protect her. But when danger strikes again, will Jack be able to keep her safe? Or will the approaching storm prove too strong to withstand?

Winds of Danger

Wes O'Neill is perfectly content to hang with his friends and enjoy island life on Lantern Beach. Something begins to change inside him when Paige Henderson sweeps into his life. But the beautiful newcomer is hiding painful secrets beneath her cheerful facade. Police dispatcher Paige Henderson came to Lantern Beach riddled with guilt and uncertainties after the fallout of a bad relationship. When she meets Wes, she begins to open up to the possibility of love again. But there's something Wes isn't telling her—something that could change everything. As the winds shift, doubts seep into Paige's mind. Can Paige and Wes trust each other, even as the currents work against them? Or is trouble from the past too much to overcome?

Rains of Remorse

A stranger invades her home, leaving Rebecca Jarvis terrified. Above all, she must protect the baby growing inside her. Since her estranged husband died suspiciously six months earlier, Rebecca has been determined to depend on no one but herself. Her chivalrous new neighbor appears to be an answer to prayer. But who is Levi Stoneman really? Rebecca wants to believe he can help her, but she can't ignore her instincts. As danger closes in, both Rebecca and Levi must figure out whom they can trust. With Rebecca's baby coming soon, there's no time to waste. Can the truth prevail . . . or will remorse overpower the best of intentions?

Torrents of Fear

The woman lingering in the crowd can't be Allison . . . can she? Because Allison was pronounced dead six years ago. Musician Carter Denver knows only one person who's capable of helping him find answers: Sadie Thompson, his estranged best friend and someone who also knew Allison. He needs to know if he's losing his mind or if Allison could have survived her car accident. Could Allison really be alive? If so, why is she trying to harm Carter and Sadie? As the two try to find answers, can Sadie keep her feelings for Carter hidden? Could he ever care for her, or is the man of her dreams still in love with the woman now causing his nightmares?

LANTERN BEACH PD

On the Lookout

When Cassidy Chambers accepted the job as police chief on Lantern Beach, she knew the island had its secrets. But a suspicious death with potentially far-reaching implications will test all her skills —and threaten to reveal her true identity. Cassidy enlists the help of her husband, former Navy SEAL Ty Chambers. As they dig for answers, both uncover parts of their pasts that are best left buried. Not everything is as it seems, and they must figure out if their John Doe is connected to the secretive group that has moved onto the island. As facts materialize, danger on the island grows. Can Cassidy and Ty discover the truth about the shadowy crimes in their cozy community? Or has darkness permanently invaded their beloved Lantern Beach?

Attempt to Locate

A fun girls' night out turns into a nightmare when armed robbers barge into the store where Cassidy and her friends are shopping. As the situation escalates and the men escape, a massive manhunt launches on Lantern Beach to apprehend the dangerous trio. In the midst of the chaos, a potential foe asks for Cassidy's help. He needs to find his sister who fled from the secretive Gilead's Cove community on the island. But the more Cassidy learns about the seemingly untouchable group, the more her unease grows. The pressure to solve both cases continues to mount. But as the gravity of the situation rises, so does the danger. Cassidy is determined to protect the island and break up the cult . . . but doing so might cost her everything.

First Degree Murder

Police Chief Cassidy Chambers longs for a break from the recent crimes plaguing Lantern Beach. She simply wants to enjoy her friends' upcoming wedding, to prepare for the busy tourist season about to slam the island, and to gather all the dirt she can on the suspicious community that's invaded the town. But trouble explodes on the island, sending residents—including Cassidy—into a squall of uneasiness. Cassidy may have more than one enemy plotting her demise, and the collateral damage seems unthinkable. As the temperature rises, so does the pressure to find answers. Someone is determined that Lantern Beach would be better off without their new police chief. And for Cassidy, one wrong move could mean certain death.

Dead on Arrival

With a highly charged local election consuming the community, Police Chief Cassidy Chambers braces herself for a challenging day of breaking up petty conflicts and tamping down high emotions. But when widespread food poisoning spreads among potential voters across the island, Cassidy smells something rotten in the air. As Cassidy examines every possibility to uncover what's going on, local enigma Anthony Gilead again comes on her radar. The man is running for mayor and his cult-like following is growing at an alarming rate. Cassidy feels certain he has a spy embedded in her inner circle. The problem is that her pool of suspects gets deeper every day. Can Cassidy get to the bottom of what's eating away at her peaceful island home? Will voters turn out despite the outbreak of illness plaguing their tranquil town? And the even bigger question: Has darkness come to stay on Lantern Beach?

Plan of Action

A missing Navy SEAL. Danger at the boiling point. The ultimate showdown. When Police Chief Cassidy Chambers' husband, Ty, disappears, her world is turned upside down. His truck is discovered with blood inside, crashed in a ditch on Lantern Beach, but he's nowhere to be found. As they launch a manhunt to find him, Cassidy discovers that someone on the island has a deadly obsession with Ty. Meanwhile, Gilead's Cove seems to be imploding. As danger heightens, federal law enforcement officials are called in. The cult's growing threat could lead to the pinnacle standoff of good versus evil. A clear plan of action is needed or the results will be devastating. Will Cassidy find Ty in time, or will she face a gut-wrenching loss? Will Anthony Gilead finally be unmasked for who he really is and be brought to justice? Hundreds of innocent lives are at stake . . . and not everyone will come out alive.

LANTERN BEACH BLACKOUT

Dark Water

Colton Locke can't forget the black op that went terribly wrong. Desperate for a new start, he moves to Lantern Beach, North Carolina, and forms Blackout, a private security firm. Despite his hero status, he can't erase the mistakes he's made. For the past year, Elise Oliver hasn't been able to shake the feeling that there's more to her husband's death than she was told. When she finds a hidden box of his personal possessions, more questions—and suspicions—arise. The only person she trusts to help her is her husband's best friend, Colton Locke. Someone wants Elise dead. Is it because she knows too much?

Or is it to keep her from finding the truth? The Blackout team must uncover dark secrets hiding beneath seemingly still waters. But those very secrets might just tear the team apart.

Safe Harbor

Guilt over past mistakes haunts former Navy SEAL Dez Rodriguez. When he's asked to guard a pop star during a music festival on Lantern Beach, he's all set for what he hopes is a breezy assignment. Bree hasn't found fame to be nearly as fulfilling as she dreamed. Instead, she's more like a carefully crafted character living out a pre-scripted story. When a stalker's threats become deadly, her life—and career—are turned upside down. From the start, Bree sees her temporary bodyguard as a player, and Dez sees Bree as a spoiled rich girl. But when they're thrown together in a fight for survival, both must learn to trust. Can Dez protect Bree—and his carefully guarded heart? Or will their safe harbor ultimately become their death trap?

Ripple Effect

Griff McIntyre never expected his ex-wife and three-year-old daughter to come to Lantern Beach. After an abduction attempt, they're desperate for safety. Now Griff's not letting either of them out of his sight. Bethany knows Griff is the only one who can protect them, despite the fact that he broke her heart. But she'll do anything to keep her daughter safe—even if it means playing nicely with a man she can't stand. As peril ripples through their lives, Griff and Bethany must work together to protect their daughter. But an unseen enemy wants something from them . . . and will stop at nothing to get it. When disaster strikes, can Griff keep his family safe? Or will past mistakes bring the ultimate failure?

Rising Tide

Benjamin James knows there's a traitor within his former command. The rest of his team might even think it's him. As danger closes in, he must clear himself and stop a deadly plot by a dangerous terrorist group. All CJ Compton wanted was a new start after her career ended under suspicion. Working as the house manager for private security group Blackout seems perfect. But there's more trouble here than what she left behind. As the tide rushes in, the stakes continue to rise. If the Blackout team fails, it's not just Lantern Beach at stake—it's the whole country. Can Benjamin and CJ overcome their differences and work together to find the truth?

LANTERN BEACH BLACKOUT: THE NEW RECRUITS

Rocco

Former Navy SEAL and new Blackout recruit Rocco Foster is on a simple in and out mission. But the operation turns complicated when an unsuspecting woman wanders into the line of fire. Peyton Ellison's life mission is to sprinkle happiness on those around her. When a cupcake delivery turns into a fight for survival, she must trust her rescuer—a handsome stranger—to keep her safe. Rocco is determined to figure out why someone is targeting Peyton. First, he must keep the intriguing woman safe and earn her trust. But threats continue to pummel them as incriminating evidence emerges and pits them against each other. With time running out, the two must set aside both their growing attraction and their doubts about each other in order to work together. But the perilous facts they discover leave them wondering what exactly the truth is . . . and if the truth can be trusted.

Axel

Women are missing. Private security firm Blackout must find them before another victim disappears. Axel Hendrix likes to live on the edge. That's why being a Navy SEAL suited him so well. But after his last mission, he cut his losses and joined Blackout instead. His team's latest case involves an undercover investigation on Lantern Beach. Olivia Rollins came to the island to escape her problems—and danger. When trouble from her past shows up in town, she impulsively blurts she's engaged to Axel, the womanizing man she's seen while waitressing. Now, she may not be the only one in danger. So could Axel. Axel knows Olivia might be his chance to find answers and that acting like her fiancé is the perfect cover for his latest assignment. But he doesn't like throwing Olivia into the middle of such a dangerous situation. Nor is he comfortable with the feelings she stirs inside him. With Olivia's life—as well as both their hearts—on the line, Axel must uncover the truth and stop an evil plan before more lives are destroyed.

Beckett

When the daughter of a federal judge is abducted, private security firm Blackout must find her. Psychologist Samantha Reynolds doesn't know why someone is targeting her. Even after a risky mission to save her, danger still lingers. She's determined to use her insights into the human mind to help decode the deadly clues being left in the wake of her rescue. Former Navy SEAL Beckett Jones needs to figure out who's responsible for the crimes hounding Sami. He's not sure why he's so protective of the woman he rescued, but he'll do anything to keep her safe— even if it means risking his heart. As the body count rises, there's no room for error. Beckett and Sami must both tear down the careful walls they've built around themselves in order to survive. If they don't figure out who's responsible, the madman will continue his death spree . . . and one of them might be next.

Gabe

When former Navy SEAL and current Blackout operative Gabe Michaels is almost killed in a hit-and-run, the aftermath completely upends his life. He's no longer safe—and he's not the only one. Dr. Autumn Spenser came to Lantern Beach to start fresh. But while treating Gabe after his accident, she senses there's more to what happened to him than meets the eye. When she digs deeper into his past, she never expects to be drawn into a deadly dilemma. Gabe has been infatuated with the pretty doctor since the day they met. Now, can he keep her from harm? Could someone out of his league ever return his feelings or will her past hurts keep them apart? As danger continues to pummel them, Gabe and Autumn are thrown together in a quest to find answers. More important than their growing attraction, they must stay alive long enough to stop the person desperate to destroy them.

ABOUT THE AUTHOR

USA Today has called Christy Barritt's books "scary, funny, passionate, and quirky."

Christy writes both mystery and romantic suspense novels that are clean with underlying messages of faith. Her books have won the Daphne du Maurier Award for Excellence in Suspense and Mystery, have been twice nominated for the Romantic Times Reviewers' Choice Award, and have finaled for both a Carol Award and Foreword Magazine's Book of the Year.

She is married to her Prince Charming, a man who thinks she's hilarious—but only when she's not trying to be. Christy is a self-proclaimed klutz, an avid music lover who's known for spontaneously bursting into song, and a road trip aficionado.

When she's not working or spending time with her family, she enjoys singing, playing the guitar, and exploring small, unsuspecting towns where people have no idea how accident-prone she is.

Find Christy online at:
www.christybarritt.com
www.facebook.com/christybarritt
www.twitter.com/cbarritt

Sign up for Christy's newsletter to get information on all of her latest releases here: **www. christybarritt.com/newsletter-sign-up/**

If you enjoyed this book, please consider leaving a review.

97046613R00194